DATE			

JURY TRIALS

JURY
TRIALS

by
John Baldwin
and
Michael McConville

CLARENDON PRESS · OXFORD

1979

Oxford University Press, Walton Street, Oxford OX2 6DP

OXFORD LONDON GLASGOW

NEW YORK TORONTO MELBOURNE WELLINGTON

IBADAN NAIROBI DAR ES SALAAM CAPE TOWN

KUALA LUMPUR SINGAPORE JAKARTA HONG KONG TOKYO

DELHI BOMBAY CALCUTTA MADRAS KARACHI

British Library Cataloguing in Publication Data
Baldwin, John, b.1945
  Jury trials.
  1. Jury – England
  I. Title II. McConville, Michael
  345'.42'075   KD8400   78–40744

ISBN 0–19–825350–8

Filmset in 11/12 point Baskerville
Printed and bound in Great Britain
by W & J Mackay Limited, Chatham

ACKNOWLEDGEMENTS

As will be apparent from each chapter of this book, we have been indebted to a great many people in carrying out the research reported here. The research, which was conducted under the auspices of the Institute of Judicial Administration, started in 1974 and the field-work was completed at the end of 1976. Throughout this time, and subsequently, we have received considerable assistance from the Home Office, who have generously funded the project since its inception. We also owe a fundamental debt to our friend, Gordon Borrie, who, as Director of the Institute of Judicial Administration, was closely involved in setting up the research and in assisting in the protracted and delicate negotiations we conducted with interested parties. Since leaving our university to become Director-General of Fair Trading, he has maintained a keen interest in the research and continued to give unselfishly of his time on the many occasions on which we have sought his advice. We are happy also to acknowledge our debt to our former colleagues, Kathlyn Bristow and Ann Keith, whose unceasing efforts in no small part contributed to the successful completion of the field-work. We could not have wished for two more conscientious and tolerant Research Fellows.

At every stage of the field-work, we have enjoyed the considerable benefit of the advice of a distinguished Consultative Committee. We would like to thank Commander R. L. J. Ashby (succeeded in 1976 by Commander G. B. Collins), Professor B. Z. Beinart, Miss E. M. Chadwell (succeeded in 1975 by Mr. N. M. Johnson), Professor W. R. Cornish, Mr. I. J. Croft, Mr. T. M. Dillon, Q.C., Mrs. S. McCabe, Mr. F. J. Mountford, Mr. C. W. Pratley, Dr. I. R. Scott, and His Honour Judge Skinner. The late Lord Justice James, who served as a member of this Committee, gave generously of his time and his untimely death took from us a dear and valued friend.

In a research project of the kind we have undertaken, we naturally are indebted to several bodies and individuals for their co-operation. Mention must be made first of the support we have received from the West Midlands Police Force and from the Metropolitan Police Force in carrying out our inquiry. We are particularly grateful to Sergeant Stuart Harris and Chief Inspector Malcolm Dines who, acting as liaison officers in Birmingham and London, carried the responsibility for organizing the complex interview time-tabling and administered between them several thousand questionnaires on our behalf. Both officers freely offered us their time and patiently dealt with the vast number of difficulties that arose in the course of the field-work. We thank them, as friends, for their selfless commitment.

The Chief Prosecuting Solicitor of the West Midlands, Mr. I. S. Manson, and his Chief Administrative Officers, Mr. N. Brown and Mr. L. Kenny, readily offered their resources and expertise to facilitate our inquiry. The diligence and care with which our questionnaires were completed are very much appreciated. We are also very grateful to the Lord Chancellor's Department for their help. We are greatly indebted to Mr. S. Carlton, Chief Clerk, and his staff at the Crown Court Centre in Birmingham who, at great inconvenience to themselves, provided a vast number of copies of committal papers, organized the administration of questionnaires to members of the judiciary and collected on our behalf detailed information on each jury in Birmingham. We were given, through the Circuit Administrator, every assistance and kept in touch on a daily basis with the progress of cases through the Court. Without this co-operation our research design simply could not have been implemented.

Many people have kindly offered helpful comments on earlier drafts of this book. We thank Professor Michael Zander, Professor L. Neville Brown, Mr. George Jonas, Mr. A. F. Wilcox, and Dr. J. P. Wilson in particular for their advice and encouragement.

Our secretary, Mrs. Ann Nicholas, deserves special mention: her indefatigability and genial disposition have made the research a simpler and more agreeable undertaking than it would otherwise have been.

Our final thanks are to our wives, Fiona and Sonia, who throughout have tolerated our obsession with criminal trials.

It goes without saying that the views expressed in this book remain ours alone and should not be taken as the views of the

Home Office, our Consultative Committee, respondents, or anyone else to whom we are indebted.

JOHN BALDWIN
MICHAEL McCONVILLE

Birmingham 1978

CONTENTS

1

JURY LORE AND JURY LEARNING

I T is customary to begin books on the jury by referring to the extravagant views that have been expressed over the centuries about that institution. Juries, it seems, provoke comments which are frequently little short of hysterical. One would in fact be hard put to it to locate within the immense literature on juries a truly moderate expression of opinion on the subject. Opponents and defenders seem to have been locked in a bitter struggle in which everyone takes sides. Despite this controversy, which has in recent years intensified, the jury system remains the corner-stone of the criminal trial both in England and in the United States. It is the existence of the jury which in large measure explains many of the procedures (that might at first sight seem archaic) that fashion the trial process and, even though only a small minority of defendants in criminal trials opt for trial by jury,[1] the right to jury trial is still regarded as fundamental in all cases involving major criminal charges.[2]

The reason the jury generates such strong antipathy in certain quarters is not hard to find. Indeed, the very conception of a jury might be thought absurd. Twelve individuals, often with no prior contact with the courts, are chosen at random to listen to evidence (sometimes of a highly technical nature) and to decide upon matters affecting the reputation and liberty of those charged with criminal offences. They are given no training for this task, they deliberate in secret, they return a verdict without giving reasons, and they are responsible to their own conscience but to no one else. After the trial they melt away into the community from which they are drawn. Put in this way, the vilification that has sometimes been poured on the jury is

---

[1] Most defendants, both in England and in the United States, plead guilty and the vast majority of cases are in any event disposed of in the lower courts without a jury.

[2] If an accused in England pleads not guilty in the Crown Court (the higher criminal trial court), he must be tried by jury. The position in the United States is more complex: see Simon and Marshall (1972).

readily understood. Oppenheimer (1937), for instance, argues as follows:

We commonly strive to assemble 12 persons colossally ignorant of all practical matters, fill their vacuous heads with law which they cannot comprehend, obfuscate their seldom intellects with testimony which they are incompetent to analyse or unable to remember, permit partisan lawyers to bewilder them with their meaningless sophistry, then lock them up until the most obstinate of their number coerce the others into submission or drive them into open revolt. (p. 142.)

The attacks that have been launched against the jury have been at all times countered with equal passion by its defenders. According to Blackstone, for example, trial by jury

... ever has been, and I trust ever will be, looked upon as the glory of English law . . . The liberties of England cannot but subsist so long as this palladium remains sacred and inviolate. (iii.379, iv.350, 17th edition, 1830.)

Other supporters of the jury argue that it is the safeguard of liberty,[3] that it is an essential check on unpopular laws,[4] that it is the best means for establishing truth,[5] and that it introduces into the law an element of community sentiment and fairness.[6] Critics claim that the jury is not, nor ever has been, any protection against oppressive government,[7] that it sometimes shows a wilful disregard for the law,[8] that it lacks practical expertise and introduces as much prejudice as good sense into its decisions.[9]

[3] Thus, for example, Lord Devlin (1956), in a celebrated passage, writes: '. . . no tyrant could afford to leave a subject's freedom in the hands of twelve of his countrymen. So that trial by jury is more than an instrument of justice and more than one wheel of the constitution: it is the lamp that shows that freedom lives.' (p. 164.)

[4] See Humphreys (1946) at p. 159, and Kadish and Kadish (1971).

[5] Lord du Parcq (1948) said, for instance, 'When questions of fact have to be decided, there is no tribunal to equal a jury, directed by the cold impartial judge.' (p. 10.)

[6] 'A jury can do justice where a judge, who has to follow the law, sometimes may not', Lord Birkett, *The Times*, 14 June 1958. See also Forsyth (1852) at pp. 430–1; Pound (1910) at p. 36; and Wigmore (1929) at p. 170.

[7] Jennings (1959) wrote that 'a jury is small protection for minority opinion' (p. 268); see also Jackson (1945) at p. 92 *et seq.*; Williams (1963) at p. 260; and Note, *Yale Law Journal* (1970).

[8] See Frank (1930) at p. 172, and Newman (1955).

[9] A distinguished lawyer is quoted by Frank (1949) as saying: 'Our own boasted trial by jury, which affirms that all grades of capacity above drivelling idiocy are alike fitted for the exalted office of sifting truth from error, may excite the derision of future times.' (pp. 138–9.)

One of the most striking features of this debate, at least until very recently, has been the basic lack of evidence adduced to support either side. Some of the questions at issue, such as that concerned with the jury as a protector of liberty, do not lend themselves to scientific inquiry. Arguments about such matters tend, therefore, to be based not upon what might be regarded as evidence but upon belief, opinion, hunch, or sheer prejudice. This in no small part explains the bitterness of the dispute and also its fundamental sterility. Other questions at issue, such as the competence of the jury as a fact-finding tribunal, seem to be questions on which evidence can be brought to bear and it is with such questions that we shall be concerned in this book. Some evidence, in the form of testimony derived from those observing jury trial or participating in it, has been amassed over the years and tends to demonstrate a general ability on the part of the jury as a trier of fact. Such material, based upon individual experience, does not allow generalizations to be safely made (except about those who have advanced the testimony) but the bulk of it points in one direction. For example, judges have been prone, virtually without exception, to assert that juries are extremely competent triers of fact. Thus, in England, Lord Halsbury (1903) said, 'As a rule, juries are, in my opinion, more generally right than judges', and recently Lord Salmon (1974) put the point even more forcefully:

A perverse verdict wrongly acquitting a guilty man is naturally galling and discouraging, but such a verdict is, in my experience, very rare. During the seven years in which I was a judge of the Queen's Bench Division, I must have presided at hundreds of criminal trials all over the country. I doubt whether I had as many as six cases in which the jury failed to convict when I thought that they should have done so. Thinking about those cases afterwards, I concluded that in most of them, there was a good deal to be said for the jury's point of view. I do not believe that, after all, there is more than about two per cent of the men brought to trial who are wrongly acquitted. (p. 5.)

His confidence that judges and barristers in general would be overwhelmingly in favour of retaining juries[10] is supported by information gathered from judges by Lord Parker.[11] Sentiments

[10] Lord Salmon (1974) at p. 7.
[11] This information is reproduced by Kalven and Zeisel (1966) in Appendix C.

of a similar nature have been voiced elsewhere.[12] Speaking of his experience as a judge in Australia, for instance, Hale (1973) said that he had almost invariably found himself in basic agreement with the verdict of the jury. Indeed, on those occasions on which he would himself have reached a different verdict, he thought the jury had, with only one exception, reached a conclusion that was entirely open on the evidence. An American judge, Hartshorne (1949), took a more systematic interest in the jury. Over a twelve-year period, he kept a record of jury verdicts in civil and criminal cases over which he had presided, together with his own opinion on each verdict. On analysis, he concluded that the jury's verdict was unquestionably right in at least 85 per cent of all cases. A national poll of over a thousand trial judges in America by Kalven (1964) provided further evidence that judges viewed the performance of juries very favourably. All this must be taken as evidence, if only impressionistic evidence, that judicial confidence in the jury has been, and remains, on the whole extremely high.[13]

Limited surveys have been conducted in the United States using subjects who had actually sat on a jury but these exercises have tended to produce somewhat disparate results. Hunter (1935), for example, found that jurors often misunderstood the relevant legal concepts and rules or else did not apply them properly. Hervey's study (1947) also showed that almost 40 per cent of jurors said that they did not fully understand the judge's instructions to them. Other researchers have found considerable confusion in the minds of jurors.[14] Contradictory findings emerged in the report of Moffat (1945), who found that most jurors appeared to understand the judge's instructions with a

[12] The present Lord Chancellor, Lord Elwyn Jónes, wrote that, in his long experience, he could remember only one case in which he had doubts about a conviction by a jury: *The Times*, 10 November 1973. Support for this position is to be found in numerous other sources: see particularly Nizer (1946); Elgrod and Lew (1973); Clarke (1975); Emmet (1974); Corboy (1975); and Joiner (1975).

[13] However, the most notable opponent of the jury was himself a judge—Jerome Frank. Frank (1930) said: 'The jury, then, are hopelessly incompetent as fact-finders. It is possible, by training, to improve the ability of our judges to pass upon facts more objectively. But no one can be fatuous enough to believe that the entire community can be so educated that a crowd of twelve men chosen at random can do, even moderately well, what painstaking judges now find it difficult to do . . . The jury makes the orderly administration of justice virtually impossible' (pp. 180–1.) Frank's views on trial by jury are summarized in Paul (1957).

[14] See, for example, Wanamaker (1937), and Hoffman and Brodley (1952).

reasonable degree of clarity,[15] and that of Brand *et al.* (1947) who noted that there was almost unanimous agreement amongst jurors that the average juror was reasonably intelligent and honest and that trial by jury produced just results based primarily on the facts of the case. No clear picture, then, can be said to have emerged from these studies mainly because such limited attitude surveys in no way represent an assessment of the performance of the jury. Furthermore, since views have been sought only from individual jurors, it is not possible to make any evaluation of how the jury as a whole regarded its task. It is perhaps not surprising, then, that this kind of survey, now very much out of fashion, has tended to produce such a confused picture.[16]

The picture is a little clearer when one examines the social science evidence which, contrary to popular belief, now exists on an immense scale. It must immediately be noted, however, that most of the research so far conducted has been restricted in scope and is of variable quality. This has been mainly due to the unique difficulty that research on juries inevitably involves, namely that all researchers have been denied access to the very subject-matter under examination—the jury and its deliberations. It has not been possible for researchers to observe jury deliberations at first hand, or even, in England, to interview jurors after their service has been completed. This difficulty has forced researchers to adopt other approaches, some highly imaginative, but it must be remembered that each method employed is necessarily indirect and subject to severe limitations. The methods that have been used to examine the operation of the jury system fall into two main categories—those that have taken the views of other participants involved in the trial as yard-sticks by which to evaluate the verdicts of the jury and those that have relied on 'simulated' juries of one kind or another. It is worth examining the more important pieces of research that have been carried out based on each method and attempting some assessment of the contribution they have made to an understanding of the functioning of the jury.

[15] See also Grisham and Lawless (1973).

[16] A similar lack of agreement is also to be found in the autobiographical accounts of jury service written from time to time by individual jurors. There is a considerable body of material based on these views and the most important sources are Devons (1965); Head (1969); Connelly (1971); Kennebeck (1975); and Barber and Gordon (1976).

6   JURY LORE AND JURY LEARNING

(1) Assessing the competence of juries by reference to the views of other participants in the trial

In any discussion of empirical research on juries, the natural starting-point is inevitably the monumental inquiries made in the late 1950s and 1960s by a team of researchers at the University of Chicago and, in particular, the research published under the title of *The American Jury* by Kalven and Zeisel (1966) which has been widely acclaimed a sociological classic.[17] This study, conducted on a scale unlikely to be equalled for decades, involved no fewer than 3,576 criminal trials[18] heard in courts throughout the United States. The researchers' approach, in its essentials, could scarcely have been simpler. It was to ascertain the views of judges presiding at these trials on the verdicts reached by the juries. The result was, briefly, that in about three-quarters of the cases the judge expressed himself in general agreement with the jury and, in those cases in which he disagreed, he was very likely to think that the jury had been unduly lenient towards the defendant in question. These results, which are probably better known and more widely quoted than any others in the whole field of socio-legal research, are derived from a massive research enterprise yet one which employs a curiously ham-fisted methodology. It would be foolish to dismiss the study because of this, but it is probably true to say that Kalven and Zeisel's study is now as noteworthy for the basic errors in its methodology as for any contribution it may have made to knowledge about juries. The errors in question have led one of the few critics of the book to observe, with some justification, that 'the bias of the respondents, compounded by the bias of the analysts, could result only in self-serving conclusions worded as confirmed proposi-

[17] Griew (1967), to take just one example, writes: '. . . I read [*The American Jury*] with enthusiasm and constant pleasure. The pattern of the argument is gently and lucidly unfolded before one's eyes . . . In this forest of evidence and argument it is well-nigh impossible either to lose one's way or to hit one's head against a tree. What is more, the sights by the way are a positive pleasure . . . It is nice to be able both to gobble the pages and to enjoy the taste as one does so.' (p. 557.) And later, 'The skill demonstrated throughout the research and analysis are such as to leave a mere lawyer limp with admiration. The Chicago Jury Project has set a standard that other inquiries into legal institutions will be proud to emulate.' (p. 574.)

[18] As a separate part of the Chicago Jury Project, the researchers examined an even greater number of civil cases; see Zeisel, Kalven, and Buchholz (1959) and Zeisel (1960).

tions'[19] and another to argue that 'the jury debate remains almost as non-empirical as it was prior to the publication of *The American Jury*'.[20] The errors, which considerably reduce the value of the study, relate to the different questionnaires that Kalven and Zeisel administered to judges (inexplicably changed mid-way through the research);[21] the thoroughly unrepresentative nature of the sample of judges and cases employed;[22] the unfounded inferences they make on the basis of an extremely limited questionnaire,[23] and an unstated, but readily apparent, bias in favour of jury trial.[24] Though these criticisms of the book do not destroy the value of the statistical material that Kalven and Zeisel present, they do nevertheless act as timely correctives to the almost universal adulation that the book has received in legal circles. The response of Kalven and Zeisel to their critics has done nothing whatever to increase one's confidence in their conclusions: rather it has served to cast their study in an entirely new, and more limited, light. They write, for instance:

Ours was a study of a large and unknown territory. Somewhat romantically seen, it was not unlike a first expedition to the bottom of the sea. There is only one way to advance our knowledge and to

[19] Becker (1970) at p. 334.

[20] Walsh (1969) at p. 144.

[21] Kalven and Zeisel state that the second questionnaire, which was considerably longer than the first, built on the experience of the first 'after considerable experience with its analysis'. The results derived from each questionnaire were none the less pooled in their analysis. (On this, see the critique by Bottoms and Walker (1972)).

[22] Kalven and Zeisel argued that their sample of judges was representative, but this claim has been effectively refuted by Bottoms and Walker (1972) who demonstrated that there was a significant regional bias amongst the judges in the sample. Fifteen per cent of the judges who participated (and very many judges refused to participate) were responsible for a half of the questionnaires returned. Furthermore, significant variations amongst the types of offences included in the sample were noted by Bottoms and Walker; drugs offences were, for instance, considerably over-represented and burglary offences under-represented. Moreover, as Walsh (1969) has pointed out, almost complete reliance was placed on self-selection of cases by the participating judges and there was no control over the time period in which the cases were tried.

[23] Walsh (1969) argues that Kalven and Zeisel are seriously misleading in their interpretation of judges' answers to essentially descriptive questions, and their inferences, upon which the validity of their conclusions rests, unjustified given the nature of the information with which they were dealing.

[24] Becker (1970) refers to Kalven and Zeisel's 'thinly veiled reverence for juries' and their 'marked tendency . . . to interpret ambiguous data in favour of the jury' (p. 329). Their tendency to favour the continuance of the jury is apparent in a great deal of their other writing.

correct whatever wrong conclusions we may have reached: another expedition that will bring new data from the depths. (Kalven and Zeisel, 1972, p. 779.)

At the risk of mixing metaphors, it would appear that, after all, Kalven and Zeisel regarded their study as little more than a pilot exercise, employing methods that were far from systematic or rigorous. Though they do not say so in their book, it seems that their book was intended merely to point the way to further research. Measured according to this limited objective, there can be no real doubt about the value of their work, though one might be well advised to be suspicious of the judgment of certain legal commentators whose almost unbridled praise of the book when it first appeared now seems to have been largely misplaced.

Before discussing in greater detail the more general problems to which the particular approach adopted by Kalven and Zeisel gives rise, it is appropriate here to examine two other studies, both conducted by researchers in England, which have adopted the same basic method employed by Kalven and Zeisel. These studies are, first, that carried out under the auspices of the Oxford University Penal Research Unit by McCabe and Purves (1972) and, secondly, Zander's (1974a) inquiry concerned with rates of acquittal in London. It is worth noting in passing that researchers in England, unlike those in the United States, have been concerned exclusively with the straightforward policy question of whether too many defendants are being acquitted by juries.[25] It is interesting that this question is scarcely even raised in Kalven and Zeisel's book.

The study conducted by McCabe and Purves was apparently conceived as a pilot exercise.[26] Unfortunately, it is not easy to

[25] This question was raised most forcibly by Sir Robert Mark, the former Metropolitan Police Commissioner, in his much publicized Dimbleby lecture. In this provocative address, which caused a storm of controversy in legal circles, Mark said that: 'the proportion of those acquittals [by jury] relating to those whom experienced police officers believe to be guilty is too high to be acceptable . . . I wouldn't deny that sometimes common sense and humanity produce an acquittal which could not be justified in law, but this kind of case is much rarer than you might suppose. Much more frequent are the cases in which the defects and uncertainties in the system are ruthlessly exploited by the knowledgeable criminal and by his advisers.' (Mark, 1973, p. 10.)

[26] This is not stated explicitly in their book but is made clear in the article by McCabe (1974) at p. 277, and in a letter to *The Times*, 19 August 1975.

make any evaluation of it since so few details of the methods used are provided by the authors. Questionnaires were submitted to counsel, solicitors, and sometimes to the judge in the case, though no information is given on how many of them actually returned the questionnaires for the 115 jury acquittals examined. However, it was apparently sufficient to allow the researchers to categorize the reasons for the acquittals. They candidly admit that the basis of their categories is subjective in that they made 'a guess at how the jury evaluated the information it was given' but it was a guess that was informed by discussions with police officers and the lawyers involved. Accepting these qualifications, their conclusion that generally 'the acquittal of a defendant was attributable to a single cause—the failure of the prosecution (normally the police) to provide enough information, or to present it in court in a way that would convince both judge and jury of the defendant's guilt' (p. 11) is still an extremely important one. More to the point, it is a conclusion which is directly contrary to the suggestion, most notably raised by senior police officers and in particular by Sir Robert Mark, that the rate of acquittal by jury is excessive.[27] According to the Oxford research, the principal reason for the acquittals was the weakness of the prosecution's case and not the result of any failing on the part of the jury properly to convict on the evidence. In the view of McCabe and Purves, only about one in eight acquittals by jury could be appropriately described as 'perverse' (by which they mean contrary to the law and the evidence). A particularly interesting question raised by McCabe and Purves relates to those cases (almost 40 per cent of all jury acquittals) that fall within their category of 'policy prosecutions' which, to use their terminology, occur when the police are pursuing social and peace-keeping policies, independently of gaining a conviction in a case. They note that, in their respondents' judgment, only four of 44 cases in this category were against the weight of the evidence, the remainder being 'pursued without real hope of conviction'. The problem that this raises, which the authors do not go into, is how to reconcile this statement with the fact that in all these cases the judge, by allowing the case to go to the

[27] See Association of Chief Police Officers' survey (1966); Metropolitan Police survey (1973); and Mark (1973).

jury, had decided that there was at least a prima facie case against the defendants in question. This does not by any means invalidate their classification but it is a question which deserves greater explanation and clarification than the authors provide.

The study carried out by Zander (1974a) was based upon the views expressed by defence and prosecution barristers in a consecutive series of 200 acquittals occurring in England's two busiest courts, the Central Criminal Court and the Inner London Crown Court. One purpose of the study was to examine in greater depth the findings of the Oxford research. This was particularly valuable since one of the main criticisms levelled against the Oxford study was that, being conducted in an area outside any major urban conurbation, it could not be taken as in any way representative of the country as a whole. The other, and main, purpose of Zander's study was to test the assertion put forward by Sir Robert Mark that professional criminals represent a significant proportion of all acquitted defendants and that they are more likely than other defendants to avoid conviction. We have ourselves been critical elsewhere of this research,[28] not only because of certain methodological limitations but also because of the definitions of 'professionalism' (based upon the length of a defendant's criminal record) and of 'serious' crime that are adopted. We are in consequence unconvinced that Zander's findings support his conclusion that professional criminals are wrongly acquitted only on rare occasions. In examining the question of acquittals in general, Zander developed a threefold classification (those directed by the judge, those that were 'perverse' or 'unexpected', and those that were 'understandable') based upon the information derived from the responses from barristers to his questionnaires. Such classifications are inevitably open to different interpretations, and we have raised questions about the way that certain acquittals were categorized as 'perverse'.[29] Having said that, it is important to note in the present context that Zander's study offers important support for McCabe and Purves (1972), particularly because he finds the proportion of 'perverse' jury acquittals to be exceptionally low.

[28]See Baldwin and Mc Conville (1974) and Zander's reply (1974b); see also Mack (1976), and Sanders (1977).
[29] See Baldwin and McConville (1974) at pp. 442–3.

The studies that have employed the general approach described here have, both in the United States and in England, so far produced results which, at least on the surface, go a long way to increase confidence in the jury system as a trier of fact. One can say as a minimum that these individual pieces of research demonstrate clearly that the respondents, whose opinions have been sought on specific jury verdicts, have by and large expressed considerable satisfaction with the decisions reached by juries in the limited sense that they themselves would apparently have reached the same verdict had they been deciding the issue. This is not of course to say that the juries therefore reached a verdict which was 'correct', though there are grounds for saying that the verdicts were eminently defensible. Furthermore, in the absence of any widespread conflict between juries and respondents in any of these studies, the results of this body of research must be taken as being extremely favourable to the jury.

The general approach based on using the views of other groups as a method of evaluating the verdicts of juries needs to be examined more critically, if only because it is broadly the approach that we ourselves have adopted in our inquiry. The principal weakness is that, as Bankowski and Mungham (1976) have cogently argued, it often leads researchers to make a number of important assumptions, either implicitly or otherwise, which are, to say the least, problematic. They write:

When the effort is made to test 'efficiency' or 'competence' it is assumed that we all know and agree upon a definition of what constitutes the 'good juror'. We would argue that no such consensus in fact exists . . . It would seem that . . . [often] the idea of the 'good juror' . . . is he who knows the law *as a lawyer*; one who accepts the prevailing courtroom norms of legal rationality and who is willingly incorporated into the social order of the courtroom and the trial. This is a view that would seem to be at least tacitly accepted by most jury researchers when they seek to confirm or deny allegations that acquittal rates in jury trials are 'too high' or 'too low'. (p. 209. Authors' own emphasis.)

We shall return to this critique by Bankowski and Mungham later in the chapter, when we shall take issue with their analysis on a number of points. In the present context, however, it is appropriate to note that the assumption that jurors *ought* to be deciding cases in ways that lawyers would decide them is questionable. Indeed, many people would argue that the very *raison d'être* of the jury is the power to decide certain cases in ways that no lawyer could. Furthermore, to use Kalven and Zeisel as an example, to say that judges agree with the verdicts of juries in three-quarters of all cases does not mean that the juries in question must have reached the right verdict in these cases or even that (as Kalven and Zeisel infer from their data) the jury must have understood and followed the evidence.[30] Perhaps the judge and jury reached their decisions in completely different ways, agreeing only in the result.

The fundamental difficulty with this line of research is, then, that it is not possible to determine, when there is disagreement between the view of the respondents and the verdict of the jury, whether or not the verdict of the jury is to be preferred. Nor can any statements properly be made about whether the extent and nature of disagreement are desirable, tolerable, or excessive.[31]

(2) Assessing verdicts by using 'simulated' juries

The use of 'simulated' or 'mock' juries whose deliberations, unlike those of a real jury, can be recorded, dissected, and analysed, has produced an enormous amount of experimental research (much of it novel and imaginative) yet all of it so obviously limited, indeed crippled, by the unreal assumptions that the researchers have had to make, that its value must immediately be called into question. There have been at least fifty separate experiments (some of which formed part of the massive Chicago research into jury trial[32]) that have been published over the past half-century. Most of these exercises have been conducted by psychologists, whose prime interest lies as a rule not in the jury as such but rather in the area of small group decision-making. It is this fact which, more than any other, has given rise to the problems encountered. The broad procedure that has usually been adopted by these re-

[30] Walsh (1969) provides an effective refutation of this argument. He writes: 'Suppose that the jury understands half the time and misunderstands the other half. Assuming that in the half they understand, they agree with the judge and that in the other half agreement is a product of chance, a total agreement of 75% would result, which is precisely what the study reveals.' (p. 154.)

[31] See further Walsh (1969) at p. 158, and Becker (1970) at p. 314.

[32] Much of the research based upon 'mock' juries which formed part of the Chicago Jury Project was directed by F. L. Strodtbeck and Rita James Simon.

searchers consists of presenting to a mock jury a reconstruction of a real trial (based upon either a re-enacted transcript or a tape-recording) and then observing how the members react to the evidence presented and how they reach their verdict. There is an almost limitless range of variations to this basic pattern, described in a vast literature on the subject, but it is true to say that most of the research approximates this simple method.

The research effort illustrates the somewhat unhappy relationship between lawyers and psychologists which has tended to characterize other research endeavours.[33] As every practising lawyer knows, the atmosphere of a trial cannot be reproduced in any adequate way in a laboratory setting and the mere act of recording or observing jury deliberations is likely markedly to distort the nature of the discussion. Furthermore, as both critics and supporters of the jury system have repeatedly argued, juries sometimes exercise in practice a degree of 'equity' in their deliberations in the sense that they may acquit a defendant whom they believe to be technically guilty in the broader interests of what they take to be 'justice'. This phenomenon would not be accurately reproduced in mock jury experiments where the fate of the defendant in question is not at issue.[34] In consequence, the experiments have built into them some bias towards jury rationality. As if these difficulties were not sufficient to undermine the studies, many researchers have compounded them by forming mock juries exclusively of students so that the resulting panels do not in any way represent the social mix which would characterize virtually any real jury.[35] Furthermore, some of the students used would not even

[33] There have been, for example, a great number of psychological experiments conducted over the years into the question of the reliability of witness testimony. Though this research has challenged many of the basic assumptions that have been made for centuries by practising lawyers, it has been treated with circumspection, if not downright scepticism, in legal circles. On this, see Greer (1971) and the Report of the Devlin Committee (1976), particularly pp. 71–3.

[34] This difficulty is of course also encountered, though not as directly, in the research that relies on the views of the other participants in the trial.

[35] Several studies have had juries consisting wholly of psychology or law undergraduates: see, for instance, Munsterberg (1914); Arens, Granfield, and Susman (1965); Becker, Hildum, and Bateman (1965); Boehm (1968); Landy and Aronson (1969); Nemeth and Sosis (1973); Mitchell and Byrne (1973); Hendrick and Shaffer (1975); and Goldman, Maitland, and Norton (1975). It is noteworthy that the Chicago research was not subject to this difficulty. (A useful review of the literature is given by Erlanger (1970).)

have been eligible by law to sit on a real jury. Other researchers have presented jurors with only written material or tape-recordings.[36] It is perhaps not surprising if, in consequence, lawyers have tended to treat the findings with a certain degree of scepticism.

Having said this, it must be recognized that the overwhelming weight of this body of evidence points strongly towards the jury being a reliable and competent fact-finding body. The simulated juries on the whole, it seems, discuss cases conscientiously, stick fairly doggedly to the evidence as presented in court, and decide individual cases according to their merits.[37] Juries do not seem, from the experiments conducted, to be swayed much by emotional or other legally irrelevant considerations. McCabe and Purves (1974), for example, in a study which involved 'shadow' juries actually sitting through 'live' trials alongside the real jury,[38] elegantly summarized their results as follows:

The members of every jury swear or affirm that they will bring in a verdict according to the evidence which has been presented to them in the course of the trial . . . There can be little doubt that this requirement seems to be in the front of the collective mind of the jury as it leaves the court, and it is thereafter not usually displaced by any other consideration . . . Time and time again, in our 'shadow' jury discussions we found that even the most errant excursus, the most uncontrolled discussion, or the most imaginative reconstruction of events, were brought to an end by a reference to what was taken to be the evidence brought out in the court room. (pp. 31–2.)

There are, it is true, certain exceptions to this pattern. Arens, Granfield, and Susman (1965), for instance, found that mock jurors failed 'dramatically' to understand judges' instructions in insanity cases, and other researchers have noted how the

---

[36] One interesting study, by Bermant, McGuire, McKinley, and Salo (1974), has shown that the procedure adopted by the researcher (specifically whether he uses audio-visual techniques, transcripts, summaries, etc. in reconstructing the trial) has a marked bearing on the verdict returned by the mock jury.

[37] See particularly James (1959a, 1959b, 1960); Simon (1967); Sealy and Cornish (1973b); Sealy (1975); and McCabe (1975).

[38] This is probably the most realistic and careful study based upon the 'simulated' jury approach so far undertaken, yet even this has not been without its critics. Sir Robert Mark, in a lecture in 1975 at Bramshill Police College, attacked the research, saying that 'academic exercises involving "shadow" juries would be laughable if they were not so sadly misleading and thus positively harmful'.

personality characteristics of individual jurors may distort their judgment.[39] But the weight of the evidence, particularly that part of the Chicago research based on mock juries,[40] suggests mock jury rationality rather than partiality.

Most of the research carried out within this tradition, both in the United States and in England, has, then, produced evidence that strongly conflicts with the general thesis that verdicts are more often determined by emotional factors or by the background characteristics and prejudices of jurors than they are by the actual evidence produced in the court room. This is in one sense an extraordinary conclusion. Much has been written over the years by practising lawyers about the critical importance of hand-picking a jury.[41] Indeed, the rationale for jury challenges (and, in the United States, the complex *voir dire* procedure) rests on the assumption that certain types of individual will be, consciously or unconsciously, more sympathetic to one side than to the other. Thus, for example, the defence may well prefer young jurors to old, males instead of females, or manual workers instead of white-collar workers. The research on mock juries, limited as it undoubtedly is, suggests that this may be no more than legal folklore. As we have hinted, however, it would be unwise to place much reliance on the research. It is probably safer to regard this body of literature as tentative and exploratory in nature, throwing up hypotheses about jury composition (hypotheses that we shall ourselves examine in chapter 6) rather than as offering any direct parallels between the laboratory and the court room.

THE PHILOSOPHY AND POLITICS OF JURY RATIONALITY

This examination of the impressionistic and empirical evidence shows that, despite differences between the jury system in England and in the United States,[42] the results of research in

[39] See, for instance, Bevan, Albert, Loiseaux, Mayfield, and Wright (1958); Boehm (1968); and Mitchell and Byrne (1973).

[40] There are numerous relevant publications here, but see particularly Strodtbeck and Mann (1956); Strodtbeck, James, and Hawkins (1957); James (1959a, 1959b, 1960); and Simon (1967).

[41] See, for example, Nizer (1946); Skochdopole (1966); Kaufman (1967); Kramer (1970); Friloux (1975); Fried, Kaplan, and Klein (1975); and Van Dyke (1977).

[42] Briefly the main differences are: (i) the interrogation of potential jurors to

both countries are remarkably congruent. In a review of major empirical studies of jury behaviour in America, Simon and Marshall (1972) concluded:

In the last two decades lawyers and social scientists have joined together in large-scale efforts to evaluate the jury system in more objective and scientific terms than had been done at any previous time . . . By and large what has been reported indicates that the jury system works well, that the participants perform their task with intelligence and interest, and that the juries' verdicts are consistent with those that experts, ie. judges, claim they would have reached. (pp. 229–30.)

The English studies broadly support this conclusion in that jury verdicts are on the whole consistent with those expected by trial lawyers. Despite the broad correspondence of the findings, however, there are considerable doubts as to both the validity and the meaning of the results obtained. It is worth emphasizing the more important problems here.

All studies have had to rely upon indirect and second-best methods of inquiry because jury deliberations invariably take place in the strictest privacy. An attempt was made by the Chicago researchers to record jury deliberations but a public outcry resulted and the experiment had to be abandoned. In England, no researcher has ever been permitted to eavesdrop on the jury and it may even be a contempt of court systematically to contact jurors after the trial[43] in the way that certain American researchers and lawyers have done. Although researchers and others have complained about this protective barrier thrown around the jury, the important point in the present context is that all studies on the jury have in consequence been necessarily limited. Apart from this general qualification, it must be said that many of the studies undertaken have greatly exacerbated the difficulties by superimpos-

---

discover prejudice or disability, a marked feature in America, is largely absent in England; (ii) fewer categories of offence are triable by jury in England than is the case in America; (iii) the English judge (who is allowed to comment on the evidence) exercises greater control over the jury than does his American counterpart; (iv) the rules of evidence and procedure differ in each jurisdiction. (See further Griew (1967).)

[43] *R.* v. *Armstrong* [1922] 2 K.B. 555, and *Ellis* v. *Deheer* [1922] 2 K.B. 113. Some have doubted whether this would in fact amount to contempt: see Williams (1963) and Cross (1967).

ing additional limitations through poorly conceived methods, inadequate analysis of results, and conclusions which tell us more about the researchers' own prejudices than about the jury.[44] How far the findings are called into question by these defects is very much a matter of judgment.

More recently, the whole empirical tradition concerning jury research has been subjected to severe criticism. In an important paper, to which we have already referred, Bankowski and Mungham (1976) argue that the theoretical and methodological basis of jury research is inadequate and that most researchers have been asking the wrong questions about juries. They contend that jury research has been mainly concerned with establishing the 'efficiency', 'reliability', and 'rationality' of juries as decision-takers in a strict legal sense. This, they argue, is particularly true in England where research has been directed towards examining the results of jury deliberations in response to the fears generated by senior police officers that the rate of acquittal is unacceptably high.[45] The fallacy in this, according to Bankowski and Mungham, is that research which attempts to dissect the jury system in the belief that the deliberations of the jury are the key exchanges in the decision-making of the trial ignores the crucial dimension of the trial itself.[46] Jurors are said to be much influenced by the judge's directions and by the way in which the trial is conducted. If, therefore, the competence of the jury is doubted, then the very basis of the adversary system is challenged. Moreover, they argue, the idea of evaluating a jury's decision is not meaningful since there is no agreement about what constitutes a 'good' juror; the lawyer's view of a decision as 'good' or

[44] The lack of a detailed account of the methodology of several studies makes evaluation impossible. In other cases, fuller accounts have merely served to reveal disconcerting limitations of design or execution and to diminish the value of the research in question.

[45] Whilst there is a good deal of truth in what Bankowski and Mungham say, it is hardly right for them to assert that there has been a 'taken-for-granted, implicit assumption on all sides (police, law reformers and researchers) that these are the only real fit and proper issues to debate and inquire into' (p. 205).

[46] They argue that: 'if the jury can be seen as a "system", or small-group, it only functions as such within the ambit of a bigger and wider system, namely that of the structure and process of the courtroom and the trial itself. And it is this "system" which provides the juror with his cues and his idea of what and what not to do in the trial.' (p. 206.)

'bad' is not the only rational or sensible interpretation.

This critique of jury research is timely and provocative. There is much truth in it though it seems to us overdrawn in certain respects. There has been, it is true, a tendency on the part of commentators and researchers to view the jury entirely divorced from the wider context of the trial, and it may well be that, in attacking the competence of juries, critics have been attacking the adversary system itself. But this does not necessarily follow. It ignores the fact that the adversary system is in no small measure the result of the existence of the jury.[47] To show by whatever means that the jury is incompetent *may* indicate, not that the adversary system is defective, but that no system can present in assimilable form complex evidence in a way that enables laymen to comprehend the issues involved. In other words, if it were demonstrated, say, that lawyers could evaluate the issues in an adversary system, the failure of the jury to do so might after all show that the shortcoming lies with the jury, not the adversary system. As has been acknowledged earlier in this chapter, Bankowski and Mungham are no doubt justified in stating that there is no common agreement upon what constitutes a good juror or a good decision. The answer, for researchers, is that any verdict should be evaluated against as many criteria as possible. A verdict is not invalidated simply because the lawyers do not agree with it; equally it is not validated by the mere fact that they approve it. On the other hand, determining whether a verdict accords with the law provides one starting-point for locating the extent of jury departure from legal rules. Such departure is not thereby approved or disapproved: evaluation depends upon non-legal criteria and the assumption that such departure is a desirable or undesirable element of justice can then be examined according to whatever criterion is deemed appropriate. At the end of the day, it may be that a jury which acts in accordance with legal rules is more desirable than one which exercises discretion in an uncontrolled and unpredictable fashion, not according to the evidence but according to its sympathies or prejudices. This

---

[47] On this, see Thayer (1898); Nokes (1956); Morgan (1956), at p. 106 *et seq.*; and Cornish (1968) at p. 80 *et seq.*

point is neatly made by Brooks and Doob (1975) in the following passage:[48]

. . . law dispensing by the jury appears to cut both ways. The fact that
minority groups have historically been unfairly subjected to jury
lawlessness cannot be doubted . . . many people would argue that the
fact that the accused is a nice fellow, a good looking woman, a cripple,
or unemployed, or that his or her victim is insufferable, should not
affect the disposition of the case . . . [Juries] are not able to rise above
the prejudices and biases held by [the average person]. (p. 180.)

We are firmly of the view that the controversy about juries
will not be stilled by any amount of evidence as to their actual
behaviour. Evidence that juries reach different conclusions
from those that judges or lawyers would have reached fuels the
controversy but does not resolve it. Those who argue that legal
experts have no monopoly of the truth would perhaps see this as
the greatest strength of the jury, whereas others see it as its
weakness. It is clear that arguments about the retention or
abolition of the jury are at base political in nature. The particular value of empirical research is that it may provide a better
understanding of the circumstances in which lawyers and juries
will differ. If it does that, it will at least impel the disputants to
make more explicit the philosophical and political assumptions
on which they found their beliefs.

[48] See also Broeder (1954); Newman (1955); Rhine (1969); Erlanger (1970); and
Note, *Yale Law Journal* (1970).

2

THE RESEARCH OBJECTIVES

THE central concern of the research discussed in this book can be stated simply: it is to try to evaluate the performance of the jury in a series of criminal trials. It will be apparent from the account in Chapter 1 that many researchers have already attempted such an evaluation and that a variety of approaches have been adopted to that end. We wanted to see whether it was possible to identify the factors which caused juries to reach their verdicts. Was the outcome, for instance, affected by the characteristics of defendants or the nature of the offence charged? Were juries commonly swayed by emotion or prejudice? Did the verdict depend upon the socio-economic background of the jurors? These and similar questions will be examined in the course of this book but our main interest lay with evaluating the verdict itself. In broad terms, the method by which we chose to examine this was based upon the views of other key participants in the trial: to pit, as it were, the verdict of the jury against the verdict of others involved in the case. Did the participants think, for instance, that the jury had returned a verdict in accordance with the weight of the evidence? What factors in their view influenced the jury in reaching its decision? Did they themselves agree with the verdict of the jury? The questions can be simply stated but the answers that we are able to provide are limited in at least two important respects: the approach itself has a number of disadvantages, and we were not wholly successful in persuading interested parties to co-operate along the lines we had proposed. Before discussing in detail the limitations of our methodology, it is important to set out the ways in which we were forced to change our original plans because of difficulties encountered in getting our proposals accepted by all respondents. Although researchers rarely devote much space in their reports to difficulties of this kind, we take the view that, in the present case, it would be seriously misleading to pretend that these problems did not exist or that they did not actually shape the character of the study that was eventually undertaken.

PROBLEMS IN EXECUTING THE RESEARCH DESIGN

The design and conduct of research often bear only a rough approximation to the textbook model of objective hypothesis-testing. Pressures of various kinds are likely to be experienced in some degree by virtually any researcher and particularly one who tackles the sensitive area of research concerned with the administration of justice in the courts. Perhaps the most potent pressure, though one that is not much discussed in the literature, concerns the possibility of conflicting objectives of the researcher on the one hand and the funding body on the other. This conflict is likely to be particularly evident when the funding body is a Government Department. The basic reason for this potential conflict is that researchers are often concerned primarily with the development of theories and explanations, whether or not these are relevant to policy issues, whereas, as Wiles (1976) notes, 'Direct government funding of research is almost bound to generate demands for investigations which have explicit relevance to policy issues.' (p. 5.) It is to be expected that governmental bodies should be preoccupied with pragmatic and political issues,[1] and this concern has to a great extent determined the nature of jury research in England. Thus, when one survey revealed a general acquittal rate in contested cases in the Crown Court of approximately 40 per cent,[2] official interest in research on juries was directed towards the relatively narrow policy question of whether acquittal rates by jury were generally too high. One danger with this approach is that, as Bankowski and Mungham (1976) argue, the scope of the research

tends to be structured by the way in which powerful opinion has, in advance, defined the precise character of the 'jury problem' . . . [and] that 'problem-oriented' research often begins by taking-for-granted the very factors that should be regarded as problematical (p. 210).

Researchers themselves, inhibited by such considerations, have come to regard the appropriateness and adequacy of Government-sponsored research in an increasingly critical

[1] Home Office interest in policy-oriented research and its practical utility is clearly revealed in Clarke (1977); Moriarty (1977); and Croft (1978).
[2] Association of Chief Police Officers (1966).

light.[3] The possibility of conflicting interests was apparent at the very outset of our research, and the Home Office, in their initial approach to us, made it clear that their main interest lay in the question of levels of acquittal. They rightly pointed out, however, that the potential scope for research related even to this objective was extremely wide. We did not wish to be, as it were, artificially constrained by narrow policy questions and, in the proposals which we subsequently submitted to the Home Office, we cast our net wide. Our proposals were not confined to an examination of acquittals, but ranged over earlier decisions taken by defendants and others in the criminal process.[4] It was also clear that cases that ended in convictions, as well as acquittals, would have to be included in any satisfactory analysis.

It must be admitted that we anticipated difficulty in reaching agreement with the Home Office over our proposals, but these worries proved to be largely unfounded. Between their first approach in January 1974 and formal approval of our proposals in July 1974 and in several meetings thereafter, the Home Office gave us every assistance in drawing up our research programme and never attempted at any stage to divert us from our expressed aims.[5] Nor did the Home Office stint in any way their financial support and, in the course of the fieldwork, an additional request for funds was readily approved. The formulation of the research design was, therefore, not subject to severe official strictures. But there were several matters that we were not allowed to examine. For example, we raised at the outset the possibility of our contacting jurors in each trial, but this was dismissed as 'untimely'. (For reasons that were discussed in Chapter 1, neither the recording of jury deliberations nor the interviewing of jurors after the trial is at present a real possibility in England.) We also advanced the

[3] See, for example, McCabe (1974) and Wiles (1976).

[4] It is well known that the sorts of cases that go to trial in the Crown Court are to some extent dependent on decisions taken at pre-trial stages, and we therefore thought it essential to examine cases in which the defendant had been intending to plead not guilty but had changed his mind shortly before he was due to appear in court. The results of that aspect of our study have been published under the title *Negotiated Justice* (1977).

[5] We did meet with an unfavourable reaction when we informed the Home Office that we intended to publish our findings relating to change of plea cases: see Baldwin and McConville (1978c).

idea of selecting a sample of cases at the committal stage in the magistrates' court, in order to conduct interviews with the police officer in charge of each case and with defendants and to submit questionnaires to the defence solicitor. Unfortunately this line of inquiry had to be abandoned when it became known that the respondents involved feared that discussing a case at that stage might lead to awkward problems at the trial.[6]

There were other difficulties that arose at this preliminary stage which necessitated certain modifications to our original proposals but we did not regard them as more than minor irritations. Our main problem was more fundamental: it was simply that of persuading the different groups we wanted to involve in our inquiry to co-operate along the broad lines we wished to pursue. In order to obtain a comprehensive view of each verdict, we sought to involve judges, barristers, solicitors, and police officers in our study. Apart from certain factual questions, we wished to ask each respondent whether he agreed with the verdict of the jury and to give reasons for his opinion. This proposed line of inquiry proved troublesome, particularly with the legal profession, and the delicate business of negotiation that ensued took up virtually a whole year. In the event we had to pursue more modest objectives (the details of which are described later in this chapter) in order to achieve a general measure of co-operation. Even these more modest proposals, however, did not prove acceptable to the Bar who adamantly resisted all our efforts to involve them in our inquiry. The Bar's refusal to participate in our study has already been widely criticized by others,[7] and it is worth stating here the reasons they gave for non-cooperation.

Copies of the draft questionnaires we were hoping to use had been sent to the Bar in 1974 for their comment. We had already been assured of full support from barristers in the Midland and Oxford Circuit (who were the only barristers to be affected by the research) although they reasonably insisted on our obtaining the formal approval of the Senate. We became increasingly

[6] It was put to us, for example, that the trial court might have been in some difficulty if the defence objected to a police officer's evidence on the grounds that his view of the evidence or of the defendant had been coloured by having engaged in discussions in a formal interview with researchers on such matters as the criminal record of the defendant or the circumstances in which a statement was made or refused.

[7] See for instance, *New Law Journal*, 28 August 1975 and Zander (1977).

aware, however, throughout the long period of negotiation with the Senate, that there was a fundamental resistance, even hostility, towards the research. We have described elsewhere the fundamental shifts of argument that we encountered, together with the many reasons the Bar advanced that seemed to us spurious in nature or else mere rationalizations for their evident distaste for the inquiry.[8] In the event, the months of negotiation came to nothing and the Senate refused to allow any individual barrister to co-operate in the research other than on a simple factual basis which would have been quite worthless to our inquiry. The agreed minute of our final meeting with the Bar held in February 1975 sets out the main reasons for their refusal. The Vice-Chairman of the Bar said that,

barristers did, and indeed for certain purposes have a duty to, form opinions on the outcome of contested cases, and that it was clear that the [researchers] regarded such opinions of great value in the research. It would be wrong, however, for these views to be made public even with the very strict safeguards of anonymity surrounding the research. There were two principal reasons for this view. First, potential clients might be deterred from engaging counsel if they felt that there was a risk that counsel might express a view, albeit anonymously, on the outcome of their case and the close relationship between client and counsel would be impaired. Second, the jury might be less likely to give credence to the arguments of counsel if they knew that counsel might privately hold a different view of the case.

Although this was undoubtedly the most severe blow to our plans, there were other problems that we had to face. Before starting the main field-work in Birmingham, we conducted a pilot study in Coventry and were able, after its completion, to clarify some of our research proposals and to refine the questionnaires we wished to use. The results of the pilot work served to reinforce our view that there were a number of issues, which we had raised somewhat tentatively in our original proposals, which would repay closer investigation. The pilot study confirmed, for example, the need to examine late change of plea cases,[9] the social consequences to defendants of acquittal as

8 See Baldwin and McConville (1978c).
9 This aspect of the research has been separately published in Baldwin and McConville (1977a) which deals with the question of negotiated plea settlements.

well as conviction, the possibility of identifying weak cases in advance of trial, and the extent of wrongful conviction. To this extent, the pilot stage was successful though it brought further difficulties in our negotiations with the legal profession. After we had completed, as part of the pilot study, an exercise which involved sending questionnaires concerned with the pre-trial preparation of cases to 25 Coventry solicitors, we were informed by the Law Society (which had given its approval to the pilot study in the first place) that it could not after all allow solicitors in Birmingham to answer the questions we wanted to put to them on such matters.[10] This was a matter of great regret to us, not merely because we were by this time almost exasperated by the difficulties we were encountering from the national bodies when lawyers in Birmingham and Coventry appeared perfectly happy to help us,[11] but more particularly because the results of the pilot survey in Coventry suggested a number of important implications for the study of Crown Court cases.[12] In the event, we were compelled to confine our questions to defence solicitors to matters relating solely to the Crown Court trial itself.

For completeness' sake, it is necessary to outline our negotiations with members of the judiciary. We met initially with the Presiding Judges of the Midland and Oxford Circuit to discuss the format and content of the questionnaires that we wished to

[10] The Law Society felt that the questionnaire trespassed on the solicitor–client relationship and that, as such, answers to certain questions would involve a breach of the client's privilege. We did not share the view but could not have amended the questionnaire in such a way that it satisfied the Law Society and at the same time retained any value.

[11] The reaction of local lawyers to our research has at other times been quite different from that of the leaders of the profession. This is discussed in some detail in Baldwin and McConville (1977b and 1978c).

[12] The responses from the defence solititors in Coventry demonstrated, for example, that most defendants were being committed for trial without the prosecution's case being scrutinized by the defence. Indeed, it was hardly possible in most cases for an adequate examination to take place because the defence solicitor had been given the case papers only on the day of the committal itself. Since in the usual case the magistrates in committal proceedings, under section 1 of the Criminal Justice Act 1967, do not look at the evidence, cases were commonly being committed for trial in the Crown Court without anyone, other than the prosecution, satisfying themselves that there was a case for the defendant to answer. We would have liked to investigate this matter further, particularly with a view to ascertaining whether any manifestly weak cases might have been terminated at committal if there had been close examination of the case papers at that stage, but we were not allowed to pursue it.

use. They asked that no question be included in the question-naires which required a judge to evaluate the propriety of a jury's verdict or even to say whether it was contrary to his expectations. It was very clear to us that many of the questions that Kalven and Zeisel (1966) were able to include in their lengthy questionnaires to judges in the United States would be regarded as improper if put to a judge in England. But we took the view that research is very much the art of the possible and thought it politic to accede to the kindly but firm requests that members of the judiciary made in relation to the sorts of questions we wished to ask. Indeed, we thought ourselves extremely fortunate to have their co-operation at all.

Our inability to approach members of the jury, the exclusion of barristers, the restricted nature of the questions we could put to solicitors and judges meant that the study we eventually carried out took on a different character from that originally intended. Although there were many disappointments along the way, we were nevertheless at the end of the day more or less satisfied with the support we had been promised and, at the start of the field-work, we were reasonably confident that we would be able to gather sufficient information to allow an evaluation of the jury's performance.

THE METHODS ADOPTED

The field-work began in the Birmingham Crown Court in February 1975 and was concluded in September 1976, during which time we collected a considerable amount of information about each case from many sources. We wanted a sample of 500 contested cases and we simply took as our sample all cases that were contested in the Birmingham Crown Court until we reached that number. Only about a fifth of all cases were contested in the Birmingham Crown Court in the study period, and we sought additional information from the police, the prosecuting solicitors, and the Crown Court authorities about the other cases in which there had been a guilty plea. The pilot work confirmed our belief in the importance of examining jury trials within the context of the judicial process as a whole and, accordingly, we sought from the police and prosecuting sol-icitors certain details about all defendants committed for trial

regardless of their plea. There were 2,406 defendants who
passed through the Birmingham Crown Court in this time, of
whom 500 (20·8 per cent) pleaded not guilty. The importance
of examining jury trials in relation to all cases committed for
trial lies in the fact that levels of acquittal following trial by jury
are intimately related to decisions that defendants take prior to
the trial, particularly the decision taken by defendants with
regard to plea.[13]

We, therefore, collected information from different groups of
respondents at two specific stages. Our main interest inevitably
lay with finding out what judges, defence and prosecuting
solicitors, and police officers felt about the outcome of cases
tried by jury. For jury verdicts in Birmingham, our aim was to
build up a rounded view of each case, the point being that, if
one gets views from as wide a spectrum as possible, evaluation
of the jury's verdict is more secure. In respect of most respondents, as we have made clear, we were not permitted to ask
direct questions about their opinion of the verdict, and it was
necessary to elicit their views by means of indirect questions.
We knew from the pilot study and from the work of previous
researchers that there was an almost infinite range of possible
explanations for any given verdict, and we attempted to provide in advance for the more important. To ensure a measure of
comparability, we sought from each respondent his explanation for the verdict in a relatively structured way, although each
questionnaire also contained open-ended questions. When a
trial ended in an acquittal, we presented each group of respondents with a set of possible factors which might go some way to
explain the acquittal. Respondents were asked to indicate
which, if any, of this list of possible factors in their opinion
might have explained the verdict and, where more than one
factor was identified, to say which factor was in their view
dominant. The factors presented to all groups of respondents in
the lists below fall into two broad groups—legal and extra-
legal. Legal factors comprise those that lawyers would regard
as relevant and proper considerations in any verdict, relating
for instance to the strength of the evidence presented or the

[13]There is a large literature on this subject: see, for example, Moley (1928); Dash
(1951); Neubauer (1974) at p. 224 *et seq.*; Zander (1974c); Baldwin and McConville
(1977a).

performance of key witnesses; the extra-legal factors would in most cases be viewed, rightly or wrongly, as irrelevant in a strict legal sense, and not appropriate considerations to influence a jury's deliberations. The factors put to respondents in cases that ended as acquittals were as follows:

—absence of witness(es) upon whom the prosecution wished to rely
—failure of the prosecution to call witness(es)
—failure of prosecution witness(es) to come up to proof
—general weakness of prosecution case
—prosecution witness(es) lacked credibility
—suspicion of apparently credible prosecution 'expert' evidence
—prosecution case rested wholly on police evidence
—police witness(es) lacked credibility
—suspicion of apparently credible police evidence
—defence evidence casting doubt on prosecution evidence
—credible explanation offered by the accused
—sympathy with the defendant
—triviality of the offence
—conduct of the victim of the offence
—other reason(s)

An equivalent set of factors was put to all respondents in respect of cases that ended in convictions and the list of relevant factors, fewer in number than for acquittals, is given below:

—strength of prosecution case
—general weakness of defence case
—absence of witness(es) upon whom the defence wished to rely
—failure of the defence to call witness(es)
—unreliability of defence witness(es)
—bad impression created by defendant
—other reason(s)

All respondents were asked for any additional comments on the case and this often provoked, particularly from the judges who completed our questionnaires, the most illuminating responses. In addition to questions common to all groups, the range of questions we were allowed to put to defence and prosecuting solicitors was less restricted and we were able to ascertain what verdict they had expected at the moment the jury retired. In the case of police officers, we were allowed to ask direct questions about their agreement with the verdict.

Though the basic purpose in contacting judges, solicitors, and police officers after the trial was the same, we employed different methods of extracting information from them. We used questionnaires to elicit opinions of each defendant's trial from the judge and from defence and prosecuting solicitors. We carried out lengthy tape-recorded interviews with the police officers responsible for the handling of each case and also with the defendant himself, though we shall not be much concerned in this book with the views of defendants. A final source of information relating to the trial came from the Crown Court authorities in Birmingham who agreed to complete standardized questionnaires relating to the socio-economic composition of all juries empanelled in the study period. This information on the background of jurors is analysed in detail in Chapter 6.

Given our general interest in examining these cases within the wider context of the judicial process, we also devised questionnaires, which were completed prior to the trial by police officers and by prosecuting solicitors on all 2,406 defendants who appeared at the Crown Court during the study period. We were specifically interested here in finding out about procedures relating to the preferment of charges and about how the cases came to be tried at the Crown Court at all. With this aspect of the research, no objections were raised about the form of the questions we wished to put. The prosecuting solicitors completed questionnaires for all cases, supplying information on such matters as the preparation and scrutiny of the evidence, and identifying the factors taken into account when the prosecution had applied for trial at the Crown Court. The West Midlands Police also completed a questionnaire for each case giving reasons for any delays in bringing cases to committal and to trial, and indicating the factors they had taken into account in deciding to charge the accused in the first place. In a separate questionnaire (dealt with more fully in Chapter 7), the police gave details of the criminal record and penal history of all defendants, together with any police suspicions of involvement in uncharged criminal activity, particularly of a serious, persistent, or organized nature.

Although information was collected on the cases of each of the 2,406 defendants who passed through the Birmingham Crown Court in the study period, the main focus of the research nevertheless concerned the 500 defendants who contested their cases. The defendants who pleaded not guilty were involved in

367 trials.[14] It is important to note here that, though 500 defendants pleaded not guilty in the Crown Court, not all of them were actually tried by jury. No fewer than 116 defendants (23·2 per cent of the sample of contested trials) were acquitted not by the jury but by the judge before the trial had run its full course. There were a further fourteen defendants (2·8 per cent) who pleaded not guilty at the outset but who changed their pleas to guilty in the course of the trial. We shall not be concerned more than peripherally with these two groups of defendants in this book but shall concentrate upon the 370 defendants tried by jury.

Apart from obtaining copies of the indictment, the committal papers, the court record sheet, and any details of the case published in the local or national press, we administered a total of seven questionnaires and two interview schedules in relation to the trial of each defendant. The very encouraging response rates from the different groups contacted are set out in Table 1.

TABLE 1

Response rates following committal and trial for each group of respondents in Birmingham

	Total number of cases in study period	Number of responses	Response rates (%)
(a) Pre-trial questionnaires for all defendants			
Prosecuting solicitors (pre-trial questionnaire)	2,406	2,288	95·1
Police (pre-trial questionnaire)	2,406	2,397	99·6
Police (criminal background questionnaire)	2,406	2,352	97·8
(b) Defendants tried by jury			
Judge questionnaires	370	358	96·8
Defence solicitor questionnaires	370	312	84·3
Prosecuting solicitor questionnairies	370	354	95·7
Police interviews	370	362	97·8
Defendants' interviews	370	265	71·6
Crown Court jury composition questionnaire	370	370	100·0

[14] The sample was not distorted by cases involving unusually large numbers of defendants. One trial involved fourteen defendants but the next-largest only five.

In addition to the work that was carried out in Birmingham, a partial replication of the study was conducted in London involving police officers from the Metropolitan Police District. Unfortunately, it was not possible to monitor on a daily basis the progress of cases in London from committal to trial, and we knew from our experience in Birmingham that, unless we could place questionnaires in the hands of judges and solicitors immediately following the verdict, it would not be worth while contacting them because of their inability to recall the details of a case after even a short lapse of time.[15] In London, we concentrated on obtaining the views of police officers about these cases, though this was, needless to say, very much a second-best procedure. Tape-recorded interviews were conducted with the officer responsible for the cases of 438 defendants who were involved in 347 contested trials. A response rate of 92·9 per cent was obtained for this group. The defendants in question formed a one in three random sample of contested trials heard in the seven Crown Court centres in London in a three-month period in 1975. In addition, the Metropolitan Police completed, for all defendants tried in these courts in the study period, the same standardized questionnaire concerned with the defendant's criminal record, suspicions of serious uncharged criminal activity, etc. as was administered to police officers in Birmingham. Altogether, 2,292 defendants were tried in London in the three-month period and questionnaires were returned by officers in 98·3 per cent of cases.

METHODOLOGICAL LIMITATIONS

It is important to reiterate various shortcomings of the methods we employed. As we have already made clear in Chapter 1, assessment of the jury's performance is an extremely difficult undertaking. Research which relies upon indirect methods must start from the premiss that no person, other than a

---

[15] We were told by members of the judiciary in Birmingham, for example, that, unless they completed questionnaires within hours of the conclusion of a trial, they would not be able to remember details of the case with sufficient clarity to complete a questionnaire on it. We were very fortunate to enlist the help of court staff in distributing questionnaires to the judges concerned. Immediately following the verdict, the trial judge was handed the relevant questionnaire by a member of the court staff. The judge then completed it and returned it to us, usually within a day or two following the trial.

member of the jury, can state what the reasoning of the jury was in a particular case. Our research, therefore, was not concerned with the actual reasoning of the jury but with a subjective evaluation of each verdict. Since evaluation depends upon inference, we thought it right to draw upon as much factual information and informed opinion as possible to support any inference we might ultimately draw. Although our basic approach was to seek opinions about each verdict from a variety of sources, it must nevertheless be recognized that some opinions are in certain respects more valuable than others. This is not merely because some individuals are more forthcoming or more discerning than others. In a real sense, we felt that the opinion of a trial judge was likely to be of greater value than that of any other respondent. The judge, like the jury, is in court throughout the trial and is required to pay close attention to the evidence given, whereas the other participants are sometimes absent for part of the trial and are not required to scrutinize the evidence closely. Thus, for example, the police officer in charge of the case will usually be called upon to give evidence himself and will not be present in court throughout the whole of the case. Similarly, the prosecuting solicitor's responsibilities often require him to go from court to court during a trial and, in practice, this means that he will often hear only part of a case. Furthermore, although it might be thought desirable for the defence solicitor to be present at court when his client is being tried, it has become increasingly common for defence solicitors not to attend the court hearing, an assistant being sent instead.[16] All these factors serve to support our general contention that it is the judge's view of the verdict, supplemented by the other sources of information, which is most valuable.

It might seem, however, that the limited nature of the questions that we were able to ask members of the judiciary would destroy or considerably weaken our approach. We ourselves had misgivings on this until we were in a position to assess the quality of the responses to our questionnaires from the judges concerned. We were delighted to find, somewhat contrary to

[16] In many cases, of course, the opinions expressed by respondents were unaffected by such considerations and frequently there were additional indirect benefits. Thus, for instance, prosecuting and defence solicitors sometimes supplemented their answers by giving also the views expressed to them about a case by counsel. Some solicitors, we were told, consulted counsel as a matter of course before completing the questionnaires.

our expectations, that judges were commonly volunteering extremely frank and illuminating opinions about juries' verdicts, in spite of the fact that no specific question was included in the questionnaire on the subject. Most of the 48 judges who participated in the inquiry (and only five refused to do so throughout the whole of the field-work) completed questionnaires extremely helpfully, and often with evident relish. We were rarely left in doubt when a judge disagreed with a jury's verdict. One judge, for example, in answer to the question seeking his opinion of the factors that might have brought about an acquittal in one case, replied tersely 'God knows!'. Others merely wrote on the questionnaire the single word 'Perverse'. Still other judges replied at length stating why they disagreed with a particular verdict. This meant that we were able to use this information as a basis for classifying judges' views of the verdicts. It is, however, important to bear in mind that, since we were dependent upon volunteered statements of judges, the extent of conflict between judges and juries in the sample may be in some degree underestimated.[17] In consequence, it is appropriate to regard the figures we present as *minimum* estimates. As we shall argue in Chapters 4 and 5, this makes the results the more remarkable.

To turn briefly to the solicitors who were involved in the research, it is noteworthy that, although the questionnaires were relatively circumscribed in scope, we were pleased to find that many solicitors spontaneously offered helpful comments about individual cases in which we were interested. Some solicitors took the trouble to speak to us about certain trials over the telephone; others offered to meet us to discuss a particular case; and a few became friends and advisers to the research. A similar situation developed with the police, where the opportunities for this kind of contact were much greater since all police officers responsible for cases in the sample were personally interviewed. Almost 700 interviews were carried out with police officers in Birmingham and London, over four-fifths of which we conducted ourselves, the remainder being conducted by our two research fellows. We rarely encountered an

[17] We were dependent on judges volunteering an explicit evaluation of each jury's verdict and, when no explicit observations of this kind were offered, we treated the outcome of the case as, in the view of the judge, justified.

officer who was unhelpful; indeed, the vast majority offered us (sometimes at great inconvenience to themselves) a degree of assistance we certainly had no right to expect.

Though we believe that the views we received from respondents were, by and large, frank and reasoned, this is not to say that the opinions given were necessarily detached and disinterested. It is an obvious limitation of our methodology that the views of respondents may often be coloured, if only unconsciously, by existing perspectives or prejudices towards or against jury trial. Virtually everyone harbours such biases in some measure: some are inclined towards sniping at the jury, others are predisposed to an opposite bias. It would in consequence be foolish to deny that these outlooks may have influenced thinking about particular trials. Thus, one would expect police officers on the whole to be more critical of jury acquittals than are, say, defence solicitors. Such tendencies are present, we suppose, to some extent in the results that we shall present in this book. We would argue, however, that respondents very commonly gave opinions that display an ability to rise above any general prejudices they might have held. This was particularly striking with police officers who frequently, when interviewed perhaps a week or so after the trial had been concluded, expressed views to us that were not merely surprising but often, it seemed, balanced and dispassionate. We quote below a few examples of such unexpected responses, not because they are typical (though they were certainly common) but rather because they show the extent to which many respondents were able to suspend their general beliefs and prejudices, and to focus their minds on the particular case before them.

Case 66 (Birmingham) [A woman police officer speaking of an acquittal in a shoplifting case] It was a just result. It was so difficult to know whether she was telling the truth. I just don't know whether she did it. I hoped she would be acquitted for her own sake. I was so pleased when she was acquitted that I could have cried. Poor soul!

Case 205 (Birmingham) [A police officer involved in an acquittal brought about by uncertain evidence of identification] I think we mainly lost the case on the identification evidence. When [the two witnesses] were cross-examined, they gave very different descriptions. Counsel jumped in then with both feet and managed to play it up to such an extent that, though the jury probably didn't think he was not guilty, there was an obvious element of doubt. Had I been on the jury, I would probably have acquitted.

Case 17 (London) [A police officer's comment in a case of attempted burglary] I've had ten years in this job and there's no doubt in my mind that the man was guilty but you've got to get it over to a jury. 90 per cent of the evidence was police evidence and the only independent witness wasn't all that wonderful. I wasn't surprised they [the jury] threw it out—the case could have been stronger, though there was nothing we could do to make it stronger.

Case 61 (Birmingham) [Prosecuting solicitor's view of an acquittal in a case involving violence] The lack of one witness meant that it was the complainant's word against the accused's. The circumstances of the case showed there may have been provocation and the defendant offered a reasonable alternative excuse for the causation of the injury. I expected an acquittal since we lacked evidence corroborating the complainant.

Case 4 (Birmingham) [A defence solicitor's comment on a conviction] The defendant, in the face of all prosecution evidence, remained adamant in his defence, which was weak to start with and became weaker as he contradicted himself in both examination and cross-examination. I very much expected a conviction in this case.

Case 385 (Birmingham) [A defence solicitor in a robbery case that ended in a conviction] There was never any doubt that the jury would convict. It was a classic case of a reprobate wasting the court's time and the taxpayers' money.

It is clear that views of this kind do not reflect the assumed biases of respondents; if anything, they run counter to such biases. It was interesting that on very many occasions respondents carefully differentiated between their opinions of particular cases and their general view of the jury system. Though it is a commonplace to observe that one's view of the particular is frequently coloured or distorted by one's view of the general, we gained the impression that most respondents were able to make a reasonably clear-cut analytical distinction in the majority of cases.[18]

Although one of the strengths of our research is the frankness

[18] Nor did it appear to us that respondents' opinions about the outcome of trials were coloured much by their knowledge of the previous convictions of a defendant where these were unknown to the jury. Indeed, over half of defendants involved in questionable outcomes had never been previously convicted.

of opinions we were able to gather for each case, a fundamental methodological point remains to be made. If, as we say in Chapter 1, arguments about the retention or abolition of the jury are primarily socio-political in nature, then it would seem to follow that the function of the jury is also in part socio-political and that, in respect of its performance, the simple criteria right or wrong, correct or incorrect, do not apply. In other words, whether respondents agree or disagree with the verdict of the jury does not make the verdict justifiable or unjustifiable: it is simply evidence that the verdict is (to others) acceptable or unacceptable. For this reason, our concern is primarily with providing a clearer insight into the circumstances in which juries and other key participants in the trial differ. In certain cases we have ourselves drawn inferences about the performance of the jury, but we have attempted to couch such evaluations in cautious terms. In the final analysis, whether the verdict of the jury is to be preferred to that of others remains a matter of individual judgment.

3

AGREEMENT AND DISAGREEMENT WITH JURIES' VERDICTS

IN debates surrounding the jury, a good deal of the argument turns on the extent to which juries' verdicts accord with the views of judges and experienced trial lawyers. In any analysis, the level and pattern of agreement will be a matter of importance for a number of reasons. It provides, for example, one yardstick by which the jury's performance can be measured, and it is certainly arguable that, where the judge and the jury agree, a defensible verdict is likely to have been reached. Moreover, the level of agreement may determine the way in which the continued existence of the jury is defended or attacked. Thus, if it were the case that the judge was almost invariably in agreement with the jury, arguments for the retention of jury trial may depend upon how far juries are seen as serving as an educative force in the community by involving laymen in the administration of justice.[1] It is important to remember that high levels of agreement between juries and, say, judges tell us little about how well or how badly the jury is functioning. This is not merely because there is no way of knowing whether the judge and the jury agreed also in their reasoning. It is rather because one needs to know a good deal about the kinds of cases that juries have decided differently. If one discovered, for example, that judges approved of the verdicts of juries in 95 per cent of cases, this might be taken, *per se*, as a demonstration of the efficacy of jury trial. If, on the other hand, it were discovered that the 5 per cent of cases in which they were at odds involved the questionable conviction of members of minority groups, or the acquittal of all murderers, this might cause us to reassess our former judgment. It is for this reason that we shall be primarily concerned in this book with those cases in which there is some measure of conflict between juries and other respondents. Part of the explanation

[1] On this, see particularly de Tocqueville (1960) at pp. 291–7.

for this emphasis is that we found a surprising degree of criticism of individual jury verdicts from respondents. This was quite unexpected because research in America and in England has, as we have noted earlier, overwhelmingly shown the jury in a favourable light. It is, therefore, important to examine both the extent and the nature of the conflict we have identified.

There is another, and more fundamental, reason for concentrating on the question of disagreement between the jury and respondents—and it is right that we state this explicitly. This relates to individual and official perceptions of the jury. If one looks at the history of trial by jury, it is clear that individual views of the jury and official policy decisions affecting the jury have been to a large extent influenced, if not determined, by various untested assumptions. We have already drawn attention to individual views of this sort but official policies sometimes reflect similar beliefs. Until 1956, for example, motorists in England who caused the death of another by dangerous driving were prosecuted for manslaughter, and it was widely believed that juries were reluctant to convict in such cases because of their disapproval of attaching the label 'manslaughter' to such conduct. There was little evidence to support this contention, but the assumption (based, as far as one can tell, on individual experience and hunch) led to the creation of a new offence, causing death by dangerous driving.[2] Now it may well be that, in the short term at least, official policy will be less affected by empirical evidence than by general social and political considerations. But it is only with knowledge of how a tribunal actually performs its task that properly informed decisions can be taken about it. This is not necessarily to say that such decisions should faithfully reflect that knowledge: indeed it may sometimes be desirable to disregard it. Whatever decisions are taken, however, they ought at least to be informed by the evidence available. By focusing attention on points of tension within the trial system, we hope to contribute to a greater

---

[2] Similar examples of these untested assumptions are to be found in the introduction of majority verdicts in England in 1967 (influenced in part by the belief that juries were being tampered with), and in the report of the James Committee (1975) on the distribution of business between the criminal courts. The latter contains several questionable assumptions, in particular that magistrates' courts are more suitable for guilty pleas and the Crown Court more appropriate for contested cases (see, for example, paras. 121, 131, and 156).

understanding of jury behaviour and to present a factual framework which at present is largely absent from the discussion. We shall, for example, examine those acquittals and convictions in which judges and others are critical of the jury's verdict and see whether these involve trivial cases or represent more serious infractions of the law that more readily give rise to concern. It is our contention that, until evidence on the sorts of defendants questionably convicted or acquitted is examined, the debate surrounding trial by jury is bound to be sterile. Furthermore, without such evidence, decisions taken about the continuance of jury trial are as likely to be based upon a false premiss as upon a sound one.

THE SAMPLES IN BIRMINGHAM AND LONDON

Before describing the over-all findings of the research in respect of the performance of the jury, it is important to give some details of the cases within the Birmingham and London samples. Table 2 provides a breakdown in terms of outcome for each defendant involved in a contested trial. The table shows that in over a quarter of all contested cases in Birmingham, and in almost a fifth in London, there was no verdict given by the jury. Some cases resulted in acquittals which the judge ordered or directed;[3] others were cases in which the defendant changed his plea to guilty in the course of the trial. As noted in Chapter 2, only those defendants whose cases were tried by jury will be dealt with in the course of this book.

It is well to bear in mind at this point that statistics on the outcome of jury trial (and particularly statistics relating to acquittals) are notoriously difficult to interpret. Even fair-minded commentators, discussing the same set of statistics, have reached fundamentally opposed conclusions. What, for example, Sir Robert Mark (1973) saw as an unacceptably high rate of acquittal by jury was regarded as unexceptionable by

---

[3] There is an important distinction between ordered and directed verdicts. If at the outset of the Crown Court proceedings before a jury is empanelled, the prosecution proposes to offer no evidence against the defendant, the trial judge is empowered (under s.17 of the Criminal Justice Act 1967) to order that a verdict of not guilty be recorded. Where the prosecution's case has begun before a jury, the trial judge may, if he decides that there is insufficient evidence on which a jury properly directed could convict, direct the jury to return a verdict of not guilty.

TABLE 2

Outcome of contested cases in Birmingham and London

	Birmingham	(%)	London	(%)
Ordered acquittals (in which no jury was empanelled)	64	12·8	14	3·2
Acquittals directed by the judge	52	10·4	51	11·6
Jury acquittal on all counts	94	18·8	152	34·7
Acquittal partly by jury, partly by order or direction	11	2·2	13	3·0
Jury conviction on all counts	209	41·8	145	33·1
Defendant changed his plea to guilty in the course of the trial	14	2·8	15	3·4
Convicted on some counts, acquitted on others	56	11·2	48	11·0
	500	100·0	438	100·0

practising lawyers, researchers, and others.[4] Another difficulty is the scope that exists for disagreement over what is actually meant by an acquittal. Defendants, for example, commonly face more than one charge and are acquitted only of some of the charges. Sometimes the conviction relates to a lesser charge and whether this should be regarded as an acquittal or as a conviction is always a matter of difficulty. Indeed, the way this issue is resolved has a direct bearing on the results that are obtained.[5] The following case provides a rather extreme example of the difficulty:

Case 243 (London) A defendant, charged with a bank robbery (involving £180,000) and conspiracy to rob, was acquitted by jury. He was, however, convicted of receiving stolen property, the value of which was less than £1.

Most people, and no doubt the defendant concerned, would regard this outcome as being much more akin to an acquittal than to a conviction. All 'split' outcome cases, however, present some scope for variations of judgment on this question[6] and there is no obvious or right answer. Table 2 shows that there

[4] See, for example, McCabe and Purves (1972); Salmon (1974); Zander (1974a); and Napley (1975). This is discussed above in Chapter 1 and also in Baldwin and McConville (1978a).

[5] On this, see the discussion in Bottoms and McClean (1976) at pp. 108–9.

[6] The official Criminal Statistics for England and Wales would, for instance, treat this case not as an acquittal for robbery but as a conviction for receiving.

were many 'split' outcome cases in both the Birmingham and the London samples. We thought it appropriate, when we encountered such cases, to classify them, simply on an intuitive basis, as cases that were *primarily* convictions or acquittals. As a rule this presented no difficulty: most of these cases seemed to us much more akin to convictions than acquittals, but a few (thirteen in Birmingham and six in London) could not satisfactorily be re-classified in this way.[7] Only nine of the 'split' outcome cases in Birmingham, and six in London, were treated as primarily acquittals. In addition to these cases, the relevant verdicts in the 'mixed' judge/jury acquittals, given in Table 2, were treated for present purposes as jury acquittals. Our purpose in re-classifying cases in this way was simply to avoid undue complexity in the analysis. We thought it better not to adhere to strict legal or statistical classifications which in several cases seemed to us unnecessarily complex and anomalous. Table 3 gives the number of defendants in the re-classified groups with which we shall be concerned in this book.

TABLE 3
The outcomes of cases tried by jury in Birmingham and London

	Birmingham	(%)	London	(%)
Jury acquittals	114	30·8	171	47·8
Jury convictions	243	65·7	181	50·5
'Mixed' outcomes (treated in this book as jury convictions)	13	3·5	6	1·7
	370	100·0	358	100·0

Having collected from various sources a considerable amount of information about each defendant, irrespective of whether the case was contested or not, we were able to examine the characteristics of all those appearing in the Crown Court both in Birmingham and in London during the study period. This provides a comparison not only between the defendants in the two cities but also between those defendants who plead not guilty and those who plead guilty. It is important to note in this

[7] In this book, we have treated all genuinely mixed cases as convictions.

context that a much higher proportion of defendants in the London courts pleaded not guilty during the study period than was the case in the Birmingham sample. In London, 55·5 per cent of defendants in the sample pleaded not guilty, whereas the corresponding figure in Birmingham was only 20·8 per cent. These patterns were not unexpected. We examined the court files for the years 1973 and 1974 in six other Crown Court centres and found extraordinary variations of guilty plea rates from court to court. Thus, for example, the proportion of defendants pleading not guilty in Liverpool was 49 per cent for both 1973 and 1974, whereas the equivalent figure for Newcastle was 23 per cent.[8] There is no reason to think that these variations can be explained in terms of the types of defendant or of criminal offences in different areas and the precise explanation remains very much a matter of conjecture.[9] It must also be borne in mind that only a minority of defendants in criminal cases in England and Wales ever reach the Crown Court, although a wide range of offences give the defendant a right to be tried by jury. For a variety of reasons, the vast majority of defendants do not exercise this right.

The decision to have a case tried in the Crown Court rather than in the lower courts is often more complex than might initially be supposed. Only one-half of those appearing in the Birmingham Crown Court, for example, had to be tried there because of the gravity of the charges they faced. It is rather surprising that, when there was an option with regard to court of trial, in four cases out of five, it was the prosecution and not the defence that decided that the case be tried in the Crown Court.[10] Thus, a comparison of the characteristics of defendants who appear in different Crown Courts in the country is limited by the fact that they may be, to a considerable extent,

[8] The equivalent figures for other courts were as follows: Cardiff 41% and 40%; Manchester 36% and 37%; Leeds 29% and 26%; and Birmingham 21% and 24%. This consistent pattern of variation in plea rates according to geographical areas of England and Wales has persisted over many years and has been set out in the Lord Chancellor's *Judicial Statistics* and *Statistics on Judicial Administration*.

[9] We have discussed this question in Baldwin and McConville (1977c).

[10] This information was supplied by the West Midlands Prosecuting Solicitor's Department for each case heard in the study period. It was not possible to collect the same information for the London sample, though we have been informed that the Metropolitan Police Solicitor's Department is anxious to have summary trial whenever possible.

reflections of the separate policies pursued by different prosecuting departments.

When the characteristics of defendants in the Birmingham Crown Court and in the seven Crown Court centres in London are compared, some interesting patterns emerge. Examining the samples used in this research (which relate to somewhat different time periods), it is clear that Birmingham defendants were on average younger than those in London. Some 36 per cent of those in Birmingham, compared with 24 per cent in London, were under 21 years of age. In both cities, there was a significant tendency for those who contested cases to be older than those who pleaded guilty. Furthermore, there was a smaller proportion of female defendants in the Birmingham sample than in London (5·2 per cent and 10·5 per cent respectively), though no tendency for either sex to be over-represented amongst the cases ultimately contested at trial.

TABLE 4

Types of offence tried by juries in Birmingham and London

	Birmingham defendants	(%)	London defendants	(%)
Violent offences (including robbery)	143	38·7	77	21·5
Sexual offences	16	4·3	10	2·8
Burglary, theft, and handling offences	151	40·8	150	41·9
Other property offences	23	6·2	37	10·3
Motoring offences	13	3·5	57	15·9
Other offences	24	6·5	27	7·6
	370	100·0	358	100·0

Table 4 shows the types of case dealt with by juries in Birmingham and London in the sample periods. There are several differences in the types of case tried by juries in the two cities which are worth noting. Table 4 shows that a much higher proportion of defendants was charged with offences of violence in Birmingham than was the case in London. (A similar difference is noted also in relation to those offences in the Courts dealt with by a guilty plea.) Roughly one-half of defendants tried by jury in each city was on trial for an offence against property. Perhaps the most curious difference to emerge relates to the differential incidence of motoring offences in the two samples, and in particular driving with excess alcohol. About one in six of all defendants tried by jury in London, compared with about one in thirty in Birmingham, faced motoring charges.

There was a higher proportion of defendants in the Birmingham sample with prior criminal records (78·3 per cent compared with 66·7 per cent in London) and more with very long records. In Birmingham, 39·1 per cent of defendants had been previously convicted of indictable criminal offences on at least five previous occasions compared with 29·4 per cent in London. Perhaps surprisingly, there was a significant tendency in both cities for recidivists to plead guilty more often than those without a criminal record.

The most striking fact which emerges from these comparisons, however, is that relatively few defendants, either in Birmingham or in London, were viewed by the police as serious 'professional' criminals. Only about 10 per cent of defendants in Birmingham (and, interestingly, only slightly more in London) were seen by the police as making much of a living out of any criminal activities, as knowledgeable about their legal rights, as prepared to resort to illegal methods to avoid conviction, and as generally showing some degree of skill and sophistication in their criminal enterprises. As we shall discuss in greater detail in Chapter 7, a somewhat larger number of defendants were identified by the police in London as being what one might call 'big-time' criminals than was the case in Birmingham. As a proportion of all defendants contesting their cases in the Crown Court, however, these represented only a very small fraction. It is also interesting, within this context, to note that the proportion of defendants, tried in the Crown Court centres in London, who had been previously acquitted of indictable criminal offences was very much higher than in Birmingham (14·9 per cent compared with 3·3 per cent). But this fact was unrelated to whether the defendants in question decided, in the present case, to contest their case or not. The vast majority of defendants who had previously been acquitted in fact pleaded guilty at the current trial. How those who fought the case fared, as well as what happens to professional criminals before a jury, will be examined at some length in Chapter 7.

THE FINDINGS—AN OVER-ALL VIEW

Turning to the principal focus of our research—opinions on the verdicts of juries—the main finding can be stated as follows: there was considerable dissatisfaction expressed by respondents about many of the verdicts delivered by juries both in Birmingham and in London. Furthermore, though there were (as might have been expected) more frequent expressions of disagreement from all groups in acquittal cases than in those that ended in conviction, there was, nevertheless, a small group of convictions that were deeply disturbing to many of the respondents, including the police.

To take first those cases which resulted in acquittal, Table 5 shows the extraordinarily high incidence of acquittals that were regarded as at least questionable by different groups of respondents for the 114 cases classified as acquittals in Birmingham. It is important to repeat that only those cases in which a statement of disagreement was made explicitly by a respondent have been treated as questionable. The mere fact that an acquittal might have caused some surprise, or have been said to be contrary to expectation, was not sufficient for us to raise doubts about the verdict. In other words, the proportions given in Table 5, if anything, underestimate the extent of dissatisfaction rather than exaggerate it.

The most striking feature of Table 5 is that the proportion of acquittals regarded as questionable by respondents is much higher than that noted by other researchers, most notably McCabe and Purves (1972) and Zander (1974a), whose work was discussed in Chapter 1. No less remarkable is the fact that the judges appeared to be wholly satisfied with the verdict in only 70 of the cases and expressed serious reservations about a substantial minority of acquittals. This, of course, runs quite counter to the public eulogies of juries made frequently by judges. It would be extremely difficult to reconcile the sort of comments of judges that were cited in Chapter 1 of this book with the frankly expressed statements of discontent that we received from the members of the judiciary who participated in our inquiry. We shall examine their statements about these acquittals at some length in Chapter 4; here we are concerned only to present the bare bones of the analysis.

TABLE 5

The opinions of different groups of respondents on jury acquittals in Birmingham

	Judge (%)		Defence solicitor (%)		Prosecuting solicitor (%)		Police (%)	
No strong view expressed that the acquittal was not justified	70	61·9	82	82·8	71	64·5	53	47·8
Some doubts expressed about whether the acquittal was justified	7	6·2	7	7·1	10	9·1	9	8·1
Serious doubts expressed about the acquittal	36	31·9	10	10·1	29	26·4	49	44·1
No response	1	–	15	–	4	–	3	–
	114	100·0	114	100·0	114	100·0	114	100·0

As is clear from Table 5, there were certain differences of view amongst respondents about the proportion of acquittals regarded as doubtful. Such differences are only to be expected, and the more important question concerns the extent to which the different groups tend to identify the same cases as questionable. Table 6 presents the results on this question.

Subjected to this rigorous test, only a third of jury acquittals in Birmingham were seen by all respondents as clearly justified, and as many as a quarter were doubted by at least three groups. We argued in Chapter 2 that there were certain good reasons for placing more weight on judges' assessments of verdicts than on those of other respondents, and, when one examines the 43 acquittals in which the judge expressed doubts about the verdict, a very interesting result is obtained. In no fewer than 41 of the 43 acquittals, other respondents independently supported the judge's assessment. Indeed, the judge's view was supported by at least two other views in almost two-thirds of these cases. We decided to adopt a working definition of questionable acquittals as being those in which the judge and at least one other respondent thought that the acquittal was not justified. This produced 41 cases (well over a third of all acquittals in the sample), occurring in 20 separate trials. This group will form the basis of the discussion in the following chapter.

TABLE 6
The proportion of acquittals thought doubtful—over-all views of judges, police officers, defence and prosecuting solicitors for jury acquittals in Birmingham

		(%)
No strong evidence that the acquittal was not justified	38	33·9
Acquittal seen as doubtful or highly questionable by one respondent	30	26·8
Acquittal seen as doubtful or highly questionable by two respondents	16	14·3
Acquittal seen as doubtful or highly questionable by three or more respondents	28	25·0
Two or fewer views available on outcome	2	–
	114	100·0

It is worth comparing the proportion of acquittals regarded as doubtful by respondents in Birmingham with the proportion seen as such by London police officers. The obvious limitation of the London exercise is that we sought the views of one group of respondents only and, according to Table 5, that group most severely critical of jury acquittals. We claim no more for the findings than that they provide limited comparative material which sheds some light on the workings of juries in London. Given that general qualification, there is some purpose to be served in making comparisons between the comments of police officers in London and those of other respondents (especially the police) in Birmingham. When this is done, an unexpected result emerges. As Table 7 shows, police officers in London appeared to be more often satisfied with the outcomes of the 171 jury acquittals in the London sample than were police officers (and indeed most other respondents) with the Birmingham acquittals. Officers in London raised no serious complaint in virtually two-thirds of the acquittals examined,[11] though this

[11] The proportion of acquittals viewed as questionable by officers in London did not differ significantly amongst the seven Crown Court centres.

does not necessarily mean that they were fully in agreement with the verdics returned.

TABLE 7
The opinions of police officers on jury acquittals in London

		(%)
No strong view expressed that the acquittal was not justified	101	66·0
Some doubts expressed about whether the acquittal was justified	13	8·5
Serious doubts expressed about the acquittal	39	25·5
No response	18	–
	171	100·0

The possibility that defendants may, in a strict legal sense, be wrongfully acquitted by jury might not of itself give cause for concern. Indeed, several writers have argued that it is at the heart of the jury's function to mitigate the harshness of certain laws or in other ways to introduce common sense and equity when the exercise of cold legal judgment would be inappropriate or unjust. There is no doubt that, looking at acquittals as a whole, respondents often took the view that extra-legal considerations did influence, and in some cases determine, the jury's verdict. In most cases, respondents identified several factors which in their view explained the acquittal, and these frequently included matters which are usually considered to be part of 'jury equity'—sympathy with the defendant, disapproval of the behaviour of the victim, and the like. Other factors that were identified included the apparent unease with which juries sometimes regard certain types of evidence, particularly evidence depending solely upon the testimony of police officers. The most important factors identified by respondents for all jury acquittals in Birmingham are set out in Table 8.

As Table 8 shows, respondents differed amongst themselves in the sort of factors they saw as relevant to a particular outcome and likely to have influenced the jury's decision. In some ways, certain differences are not important. Thus, for example, some respondents might identify a weakness on the prosecution side whereas other respondents, in the same case, might see the defence side as being strong. Little turns upon such differences since a jury's decision will in many trials be based on the relative merits of the prosecution and defence cases and often the sides are finely balanced. If the prosecution evidence is weak, the defence case may appear strong by comparison. Perhaps the most striking difference, as Table 8 shows, is that defence solicitors, unlike other respondents, saw extra-legal factors affecting the outcome in only a very small number of trials. The power of the jury to mitigate the harshness of the law in individual cases is a contentious question and we shall examine in Chapter 4 the trials which ended in questionable acquittals in order to ascertain whether or not they can be said to represent instances of this equitable function of the jury.

TABLE 8

Most important factor identified in jury acquittals in Birmingham by different respondents

	Judge (%)		Defence solicitor (%)		Prosecuting solicitor (%)		Police (%)	
Some weakness in prosecution case	29	25·7	49	49·5	21	19·1	32	28·9
Strength of the defence case	35	31·0	36	36·4	37	33·6	30	27·0
Jury mistrust of the type of prosecution evidence	7	6·2	7	7·1	4	3·6	9	8·1
Jury swayed by sympathy with defendant or antipathy to victim	28	24·8	4	4·0	41	37·3	29	26·1
Other factors	5	4·4	2	2·0	6	5·5	9	8·1
No factor identified as relevant	9	7·9	1	1·0	1	0·9	2	1·8
No response	1	–	15	–	4	–	3	–
	114	100·0	114	100·0	114	100·0	114	100·0

Whether one views acquittals produced solely by equitable considerations as justified or not, the alternative possibility of juries exercising their power in the opposite direction, by convicting defendants on the basis of poor judgment, ignorance, or prejudice, is quite indefensible. Yet, in principle, that possibility certainly exists, not only because juries (like other triers of fact) may make mistakes but also because, once one recognizes the power of the jury to acquit a guilty defendant on the basis of extra-legal considerations, one must admit the corollary that verdicts may sometimes be based upon intolerance or bias. Although we cannot ever be sure whether any innocent persons were convicted in the trials within the present samples, there was nevertheless among both the Birmingham and the London cases a small number of convictions about which respondents expressed grave misgivings. It is right to stress that the vast majority of convictions were viewed as well justified by judges, police officers, and solicitors, but there remains a group, representing perhaps 5 per cent, or even 10 per cent, of all cases that resulted in convictions, in which disturbing doubts were raised by respondents about the verdict returned.

When we decided to examine convictions by jury, we were unsure what to expect. In America, Kalven and Zeisel (1966) had found that the trial judge would have acquitted in about 3 per cent of cases where the jury convicted,[12] but no comparable systematic study of convictions has ever been undertaken in England.[13] We thought it probable that few, if any, convictions would be seriously questioned, the more so because of the high standard of proof that the prosecution must discharge in criminal cases. This anticipated reluctance of respondents to question convictions might be thought to justify giving added weight to any doubts actually expressed, but we decided to treat opinions on convictions in more or less the same way as those on acquittals. Moreover, the limited nature of the questions we were permitted to ask respondents demanded caution. Thus, the mere fact that respondents said that they had been uncertain of the outcome or that they had expected an acquittal did not, of itself, justify questioning any conviction. Only in those cases in which information was given detailing doubts in explicit terms have we thought it right to raise the possibility of

[12] Kalven and Zeisel (1966) at p. 58.

[13] There are, of course, several examinations of the problem of wrongful convictions, but these are generally confined to individual cases. See especially on this Brandon and Davies (1973).

a questionable conviction. Taking into account these qualifications, Table 9 sets out the results on this question.

TABLE 9
Over-all views of judges, police, defence and prosecuting
solicitors on jury convictions in Birmingham

		(%)
Conviction not doubted by any respondent	222	88·4
Conviction doubted by one respondent	6	2·4
Conviction doubted by two respondents	8	3·2
Conviction doubted by three respondents	4	1·6
Conviction doubted by all four respondents	3	1·2
A great deal of uncertainty about the conviction	8	3·2
Too few views available to classify the outcome	5	–
	256	100·0

These broad results will be examined in greater detail in Chapter 5,[14] but it must be stressed at this point that our information on questionable convictions can only be regarded as tentative. Any observer of the legal system in England knows that, even when a defendant has been wrongfully convicted, it may take years of painstaking effort to establish that there has been a miscarriage of justice. The information we have collected on this subject is not such as to reveal demonstrable injustices in this way; rather it serves to raise questions about the accuracy of juries as a means of convicting only the genuinely guilty.

[14] As we shall discuss in Chapter 5, doubts about the conviction were expressed by police officers in London in ten cases.

4

QUESTIONABLE ACQUITTALS BY JURY

We indicated in the previous chapter that the proportion of cases tried by jury in Birmingham resulting in verdicts that were at least doubtful was much higher than one might have expected from the available literature on the subject. Not only have lawyers, and particularly judges, for centuries written in an almost lyrical manner about juries, but their views have in large measure been supported, if in a more prosaic vein, by numerous pieces of empirical research undertaken over the past thirty years. The lack of congruence between this body of writing and the results of our own research calls for some explanation. This is not easy to offer though some matters are obviously relevant. As already discussed, we were able to avoid some of the methodological defects that have beset earlier research and can claim at least to have gathered a wider range of opinion for every jury verdict examined than has been obtained by other researchers. Because of this, our sample of questionable verdicts includes only those cases in which there is a certain measure of consensus amongst respondents that the verdict was dubious. In principle it is unsatisfactory to rely on one view alone and the crux of our research methodology hinges on our success in building a 'rounded' view of each acquittal, using the judge's opinion as the starting-point. Although the proportion of acquittals we classify as questionable (36 per cent) is much higher than other researchers have found in the past, it is important to stress that the measures we used are likely, if anything, to underestimate the extent of disagreement. This is because we have had to rely to a considerable degree on respondents spontaneously mentioning the fact that they disagreed with a particular verdict (since we were not always able to ask direct questions about this) and, only then, when their disagreement was made explicit.

We have argued earlier that much of the research on juries must be read with an eye to the researcher's own implicit or

disguised biases in favour of the jury system.[1] This is not to say
that the writers concerned have been misguided or in any way
dishonest, but rather that, in virtually any piece of social
research, no one can remain objective and neutral when inter-
preting the results.[2] This probably applies more strongly to
research concerned with juries than to almost any other area of
inquiry, and the significance and interpretation of particular
findings are very largely a matter of individual judgment. As we
have seen, different observers have derived different conclusions from essentially the same information, and these conclusions in some measure tend to reflect the observer's stated and
unstated biases. It is right to point out that we ourselves began
our inquiry with an expectation that the results would on the
whole prove favourable to the system of trial by jury. This
expectation has been dashed by the results we have unearthed
and it is important to present a good deal of the qualitative
material that we have collected during the course of the field-
work. In this way, we attempt to offer a basis for an adequate
assessment both of the validity of the tables presented in Chapter 3 and of our general conclusion that juries reached, with
considerable frequency, verdicts that could not be regarded as
true verdicts according to the evidence.

We have deliberately avoided using the term 'perverse' to
describe the 41 acquittals we shall examine in this chapter
because the term is not free from ambiguity. The term might
simply mean that the verdict was contrary to the weight of the
evidence and, in legal terms, indefensible, though some writers
would not regard such a verdict as perverse if it can be supported on non-legal grounds. When, therefore, a respondent
described a verdict as 'perverse', it is not clear which meaning
was intended. Since the term requires a precision of judgment
that, given the nature of the information available to us, we
cannot claim to have exercised, we shall avoid its use. Our
concern, in any event, is more with probabilities than with
definite or clear-cut categories. If, for example, judges, police

---

[1] See, for instance, Becker (1970) at p. 329 and Baldwin and McConville (1974).

[2] Howard Becker (1967) states the problem as follows: 'Almost all the topics that
sociologists study, at least those that have some relation to the real world around us, are
seen by society as morality plays and we shall find ourselves, willy-nilly, taking part in
those plays on one side or the other.' (p. 245.)

officers, and solicitors (who do not after all carry the responsibility that the jury carries for the accused's fate) are all agreed that a particular case has been decided wrongly, this in itself does not make the outcome 'perverse': rather we argue that it raises questions and doubts about the verdict. At the very least, it suggests that other forms of tribunal might well have decided the case differently. We have in consequence tried to avoid assessments of verdicts as right or wrong, or as perverse or otherwise, and have confined ourselves to a weaker and more fluid terminology. Everything depends upon definition, and different researchers (and other observers) would by no means necessarily agree with the definitions we have adopted. Almost two-thirds of all jury acquittals in Birmingham were regarded as doubtful by at least one respondent, whereas no more than a handful was doubted by all of them. Deciding upon a satisfactory working definition of doubtful acquittals, therefore, presents enormous scope for individual variations of judgment. For the reasons given in Chapter 3, we chose a definition based upon the disagreement voiced by the judge in any case, coupled with that of at least one other respondent. This produced 41 questionable acquittals—36 per cent of all jury acquittals in Birmingham.[3] When the judge himself expressed no contrary view, we did not treat an acquittal as questionable, even if several other respondents raised doubts about it. Since we regard the views of members of the judiciary as of primary importance in our classification of acquittals, it is necessary to start by setting out a few of their comments about the acquittals in the Birmingham sample so as to give some idea of the frankness of their opinions:[4]

Case 264 [A case of an employee charged with stealing money from a till]

Judge: The jury returned a wrong verdict in my opinion—due to sympathy with the accused and *not* according to the evidence.

[3] Different measures would of course produce different numbers of questionable acquittals, though there is a fairly high degree of consensus about the 41 cases examined here. If, for example, we had included all cases doubted by at least two respondents (regardless of whether one was the judge or not), this would have produced only four more questionable acquittals than the present measure. Furthermore, it is important to note that two-thirds of the 41 cases were doubted by at least three of the four respondents.

[4] In all cases discussed in the text, any detail that might identify any individual concerned has been disguised.

Case 266 [A case involving a fight at a football match]
Judge: The verdict was in my view quite contrary to the evidence.

Cases 470–3 [A case involving four men who were said to have attacked a bus conductor]
Judge: I am quite unable to say why the jury acquitted. I thought the prosecution evidence was overwhelming.

Case 477 [A simple case of stealing from a cloakroom]
Judge: My comment would be that the verdict was perverse. The accused was caught red-handed by two police officers. He had a bad record of dishonesty—of which of course the jury was unaware—and he 'staged' (as I thought) an outburst of tears in the course of cross-examination.

These views are forthright and unambiguous; they show that the judges in question strongly disagreed with the verdicts of the jury and suggest that, had they been trying the case without a jury, the judges themselves would have convicted. It is of course arguable that such views tell us as much about the judge concerned as they do about the juries; that is to say, these may be expressions of opinion by judges who have little experience of, or faith in, jury trial. We considered this argument but found that it was not sustained by the evidence. In all, twelve different judges identified acquittals as questionable and it would not be correct to assume that these judges held views that were in general unfavourable to the jury system. In fact, these twelve judges were together responsible for completing over three-quarters of all the questionnaires returned by the judiciary and, in most cases over which they presided, they did not express any dissatisfaction whatsoever with the verdicts returned. As to experience, about 80 per cent of the verdicts in question were doubted by highly experienced, full-time judges. Despite the experience and apparent detachment of the judges concerned, we felt it important to weigh adverse opinions of the judge against the comments of other respondents, and we give below five examples of judicial criticism of acquittal cases together with the doubts that were expressed about the same cases by other respondents:

Case 59 [A case in which the defendant was charged with stealing property, valued at £50, from an antique shop]

Judge: The prosecution case was very strong. The defendant completely denied the offence. A magistrates' court would certainly
have convicted.

Police: Three of our witnesses were good average witnesses and one
was described by the prosecution barrister as one of the best he had
ever seen. I was very surprised by the verdict. On the evidence, it
was wrong. It shows the present malfunctioning of the system.
According to the evidence, he was clearly guilty.

Case 84 [A case involving a serious assault on a police officer]

Judge: This verdict was wholly perverse. The defendant was a physi-
cally small man who, unknown to the jury, had a history of mental
instability and violence. No real defence was advanced.

Defence solicitor: Personally I cannot determine any reasonable
explanation for his acquittal. The defendant is a violent man and I
am quite sure the acquittal was not in his best interests. He is
rapidly deteriorating mentally and needs psychiatric treatment.

Police: The defendant never disputed the offence or the evidence of
the police officers. His explanations in court were those of a
deranged man. It was the worst verdict I have ever been involved
with—there was no way in which the jury should have found him
not guilty. Everyone who had any dealings with him felt he should
be in a mental hospital.

Case 175 [A 'mugging' case involving a small sum of money from a
housewife]

Judge: Perverse verdict.

Defence solicitor: There is no factor which explains this acquittal and
it may be said it was due to the jury.

Police: The verdict was shocking to everyone in court.

Case 261 [A case of violence against two other men]

Judge: I have no idea why the jury acquitted. I thought [the prosecution witnesses] gave their evidence clearly and impressively. The
defendant accused them of conspiracy and perjury without the
slightest justification for such allegations.

Prosecuting solicitor: The defendant admitted causing the injuries
but stated he was set about first. He is a violent man who has
already served prison sentences for violence. The jury must have
believed his story although there was overwhelming prosecution
evidence.

Police: On the evidence, and provided that the jury acted reasonably,
he should have been convicted. I think the verdict was wrong, the
evidence was most clear. If the jury considered the evidence and

nothing else, they would have had to have found him guilty. The verdict they returned was perverse.

Cases 460–1 [Cases which involved two men who were accused of stealing property from a shop. They were detained after being chased by the police with the property in their possession.]

Judge: I cannot say why the jury acquitted. The verdict appeared to be quite contrary to the evidence. In any event, the defendants were most unimpressive witnesses.

Police: I thought the verdicts were wrong, very poor. I didn't think that a jury could be so gullible.

One very interesting feature of these 41 questionable acquittals was that, although we were successful in obtaining interviews with 71·6 per cent of the defendants involved in jury trials in Birmingham,[5] we found that defendants who were said to have been acquitted in questionable circumstances were curiously elusive or else unwilling to be interviewed. Indeed, in only about 40 per cent of these cases did we succeed in interviewing the defendant, and, in as many as a half of these cases, this was probably only because the defendant had been subsequently sentenced to a term of imprisonment for another offence and, on that account, was more likely to agree to be interviewed.[6] In some of these cases at least, it is hard to resist the suspicion that our signal lack of success in obtaining interviews with the defendants in question indicated that they might well have had something to hide. Although this inference is obviously only conjectural, the low response does suggest that these cases *were* different in several respects from other acquittals within the sample, independently of any view expressed about them by respondents. It is worth examining these cases in more detail to discover whether any distinctive characteristics account for the acquittals.

If a jury returns a verdict of acquittal against the weight of the evidence, it may be that there are certain features of the case which give rise to a degree of sympathy for the defendant. Where such factors are present, it is often argued that it is in the interests of fairness or equity that the jury acquit in the teeth of the evidence. There is a sizeable literature, and a fierce

---

[5] We achieved a higher response rate (81 per cent) with those defendants who were involved in late changes of plea cases; see here Baldwin and McConville (1977a).

[6] See Baldwin and McConville (1977a) at pp. 4–5.

unresolved controversy, on the general question whether juries should always deliver a verdict in accordance with the evidence or whether part of their function is to temper the harshness and rigidity of the law by being, as it were, the 'moral conscience' of the community in particular cases.[7] Brooks and Doob (1975) put the problem as follows:

Whatever role the jury has in theory, in practice it is clear that the jury can ignore the strict application of the law and respond to the unique aspects of each case that comes before it. The jury deliberates in secrecy, they do not give reasons for their verdict, they are in no way accountable for their verdict, their decisions do not establish a precedent that is binding on future cases, and in criminal cases if the jury acquits the accused their decision is final. Indeed the jury's right to determine the facts gives them an almost unlimited discretion in returning whatever verdict they choose. (p. 174.)

How far the questionable acquittals in the present sample fell within the category of 'equity' verdicts is to a certain extent a matter of speculation. Since we were not ourselves present in court to hear the evidence in more than a small number of cases, it is extremely difficult for us to form any precise view on this question. We noted in the previous chapter that respondents commonly saw juries' verdicts as swayed by factors which, in a strict legal sense, would undoubtedly be considered irrelevant to the proper determination of the case, for instance a degree of sympathy for the accused or antipathy for the victim. Whether juries are generally justified in acting upon such considerations requires a value judgment that we are not strongly placed to exercise. We shall instead confine our attention to describing the kind of cases that appear to have ended as questionable acquittals. It must immediately be stated that, although there were some cases within this group in which an element of sympathy for the defendant might have been influential, there are many more comparable cases that resulted in convictions where the jury did not appear to be similarly influenced. This makes it extremely difficult to identify any patterns amongst the questionable acquittals either in terms of the sort of offences alleged or the type of individuals on

[7] See on this question, Pound (1910); Wigmore (1929); Frank (1930); Broeder (1954); Kalven (1964); Kalven and Zeisel (1966); Van Dyke (1970); Kadish and Kadish (1971); Note in *Yale Law Journal* (1974); and Brooks and Doob (1975).

trial. The three following examples, which could conceivably be classified as 'equity' verdicts, gave rise to considerable differences of view amongst the various respondents:

Case 6 [A case in which a youth was apprehended whilst acting as look-out for two others who had broken into a warehouse. The two others ran off and were never caught. The youth said he knew nothing at all about the burglary.]

Judge: A lawyer wouldn't have believed the story but the layman clearly could and did.

Prosecuting solicitor: The verdict was incomprehensible to me.

Police: I feel that if we had arrested the two co-defendants, there would have been a different outcome to the case.

Case 119 [A case of an employee in a store said to have stolen a small sum of money. He had worked at the same store for over 20 years. A trap had been laid after large sums of money had gone missing and he was apprehended as a result.]

Judge: The jury may well have thought that this amateur detective work, especially when carried out by colleagues and persons known to the defendant, should not be encouraged. They acquitted in this case, despite the prosecution evidence which on the face of it was strong, because of sympathy for the defendant, especially having regard to his age and [lack of] record and to the probable consequences of a conviction.

Police: He tried to create an image of a docile old man being victimized for less than £5. The barrister did a fantastic job with this. But I thought we'd get the case home no bother at all, I honestly did. I'm still very surprised about it, even knowing his defence. You get this in cases where a defendant has worked for the same firm for years and years. He's getting on a bit and he'd lose his job—all for £4.

Cases 419–22 [A case of four men involved in a violent altercation when the victims' behaviour was to some extent provocative]

Judge: This was a *very* unusual case. The jury felt that it served [the victims] right. They sympathized with the accused and were ready to accept their rather facile explanations.

Prosecuting solicitor: A sympathy verdict.

Defence solicitor: As the trial wore on, the attitude of the jury seemed to be informed scepticism of the prosecution evidence rather than not listening to it. I would not regard it at all as a sympathy verdict. I take the view that on the day, the defendants were entitled to the acquittal they received—particularly on the evidence.

Police: A reasonable jury must have returned a verdict of guilty in this
case. I think it's right to say that the prosecution case was absolutely overwhelming. Without the slightest doubt, these acquittals
were perverse—I can't see any legal justification whatsoever for
them. I thought at one time that when one looked at the evidence
and weighed it up, we might have expected a plea of guilty with
some very strong mitigation. I think the defence were banking on a
sympathy verdict and this they got.

In each of these cases the verdicts returned might be regarded
as 'equitable' in the sense that, although respondents by and
large thought the defendants technically guilty, the jury's verdict was in some degree defensible. Whatever one's view about
such cases, however, it was pretty clear to us that relatively few
of the questionable acquittal cases were of this kind. Almost as
frequent as the 'equity' cases were those at the other end of the
scale where apparently dangerous criminals were acquitted.[8]
The following comment by a police officer, though not by any
means typical of acquittals within this group, suggests that a
jury's acquittal may on occasion have alarming consequences:

Cases 274–7 [A case involving the acquittal—described by the judge in
the case as 'incredible'—of four armed robbers]
Police: There was all the evidence in the world—in fact, their defence
was laughable. I was absolutely flabbergasted when they were
acquitted because I know that they're violent men and I think that,
if we hadn't been there that night, someone would have been
seriously injured or killed. I'm quite convinced of that.

The accepted view is that juries are particularly prone to
acquit against the weight of the evidence in a number of clearly
identifiable instances. Motoring offences are the most obvious
example, where the alleged difficulty in getting juries to convict
transparently guilty people has attracted criticism from police,
lawyers, and judges. Juries are also said to have a distaste for
certain laws, particularly laws touching upon the area of public
morality, such as obscene publications laws, and to show this
distaste by over-readily acquitting. There is also evidence that
juries may be reluctant to convict in cases involving domestic
violence where they may feel that matters can be resolved more

[8] This is exactly the sort of case referred to by Sir Robert Mark (1973) in his
comments on defects of the English criminal justice system. We shall examine the
question of how 'professional' criminals fare before juries in Chapter 7.

satisfactorily by other procedures.[9] Not all allegations of this over-readiness to acquit assume that the decision of the jury is a conscious one: whenever a trial is of a technical or complex nature (as in fraud cases) or the proceedings protracted and involved, there is said to be a real danger that the jury will acquit merely because it has become confused.[10] All these beliefs are well known and widely expressed, yet a striking feature of the 41 cases is that very few fell within any of these categories. None of them, for example, involved motoring or public morality offences. All the acquittals related in fact to fairly straightforward property, violent, or sexual offences. What seems to have happened on other occasions, when one might have suspected a strong element of jury equity, was that respondents eschewed making any adverse judgment of the verdict returned and, in consequence, we classified the acquittal as justifiable. The following comments illustrate the point in relation to one such case:

Case 323 [An obscenity trial]
Judge: Matter of opinion on public morals.
Prosecuting solicitor: The verdict probably reflected changing public attitudes to obscenity and the portrayal of sexual activities.
Police officer: I expected an acquittal here because of the general trend of tolerance and permissiveness. I take a different view on these matters myself.

Since such cases were not, therefore, within the questionable acquittal group, it would be very difficult in our judgment to maintain that any of the 41 cases represented instances of juries taking a dislike to laws out of line with general community sentiment.[11] Furthermore, not one of the questionable acquittals involved complex frauds, offences which were rarely contested before juries in Birmingham during the study period. Indeed, of the eight cases of fraud which raised questions of

---

[9] See, for example, McCabe and Purves (1972) p. 33.

[10] See, for instance, a leading article in *The Times*, 11 January 1973, which generated a good deal of correspondence: 'There is a strong case . . . for removing from juries complicated frauds and other cases turning on intricate financial transactions. It is extremely doubtful whether jurors can adequately follow the detailed and difficult evidence which is so often necessary in cases of this type.'

[11] As is apparent from the examples cited, there are some cases when the jury might have regarded the application of some laws as unduly harsh in particular instances; examples of this are provided by *cases 119* and *419–22* cited on pp. 59–60

some complexity, six resulted in the defendants being convicted and the two acquittals were regarded as broadly justified by respondents.[12] Nor were many of the questionable acquittals the result of lengthy or involved trials; most of them were, on the contrary, relatively short and straightforward cases. Finally, only one of the 41 defendants was involved in a case involving domestic violence.

Despite the controversy about jury equity, it was apparent, then, that few of the questionable acquittals by juries in Birmingham could be attributed to that factor. The truth is that we could not detect any common characteristics amongst these cases and, indeed, found many more cases amongst the convictions in the Birmingham sample in which some measure of jury equity would have been more easily justified.

We have been concerned so far in this chapter with the outcome of acquittals in Birmingham, and it is important now to attempt to ascertain how far the limited information obtained from police officers in London confirms these results. We noted in Chapter 3 that officers in London were on the whole less critical of jury verdicts than officers in Birmingham. This is a quite remarkable difference, not least because the jury acquittal rate in London was much higher than the corresponding rate in Birmingham (47·8 per cent and 30·8 per cent respectively).[13] If we examine the cases of those 39 acquitted defendants (involved in 29 separate trials) about which London officers expressed strong criticisms, it is apparent that an essentially similar picture emerges. Again there is no obvious or clear-cut pattern either in terms of the nature of the offences charged or of the defendants tried. It seemed that in London, as

[12] A senior police officer, interviewed in connection with an extremely complex fraud case in which the defendant was convicted, made the following interesting observation: 'I don't think we need special tribunals for this kind of case, because all my experience has been that juries are sufficiently mentally aware to see where there has been a "rip-off". I have no complaints about the way juries have dealt with any of my cases. I used to think you'd need a jury of stockbrokers, bank managers and accountants to get a conviction but now I realize you don't need detectives who have been bank managers, stockbrockers or accountants to investigate these cases. All you need are sensible people who can tell when there's a "rip-off".'

[13] It is also pertinent to note that Sir Robert Mark, who delivered a fierce attack in 1973 on juries and on the tactics employed by defence lawyers in jury trials, was the Commissioner of the Metropolitan Police Force throughout the time of the research. We are ourselves heavily indebted to Sir Robert for affording us every facility to conduct our research in London.

in Birmingham, the unexpected benefits to defendants which appeared to arise as a result of the vagaries of trial by jury tended to fall rather randomly. It is true that there were several cases which might be regarded as 'jury equity' acquittals and others in which the jury might reasonably have felt a degree of sympathy for the defendant, but it seemed to us that no more than a small minority were genuine examples of this kind. There is, however, a fairly broad 'grey' area of cases in which the officer thought that an element of sympathy might have been shown for the defendant though in his opinion this had been largely misplaced. A couple of examples will make this distinction clear. In *cases 29–30*, two youths were acquitted, despite strong prosecution evidence, in a case in which a homosexual was badly beaten and robbed of over £100 worth of property. In the view of the officer, the explanation for the acquittal lay in the jury's distaste for the victim's character. Similarly, in *case 242*, the girl-friend of a man who had been convicted of a number of serious burglaries was acquitted of handling some of the property. According to the officer, the evidence against her was virtually as strong as the evidence against her boy-friend, and he observed that 'her counsel played on the sympathy angle, saying she was under the domination of her boy-friend'.

There is one interesting difference in the pattern of acquittals regarded as questionable by London officers compared to that found in Birmingham. This relates to the type of offences with which the defendants in question had been charged. Whereas all questionable acquittals in Birmingham involved violent, sexual, or property offences, only slightly more than one-half of those in London did so. There were, for example, six defendants in London involved in five separate cases of possessing cannabis, four others acquitted of gross indecency as well as two cases of causing death by dangerous driving (jury equity cases, *par excellence*). Though our information on the subject is limited,[14] it seems likely that the differences between London and Birmingham cases in this regard are to be explained much

---

[14] Offences relating to indecency, drugs, and causing death by dangerous driving were not contested with sufficient frequency in either city to allow any generalizations to be drawn about the propensities of juries to acquit or to convict in offences of this kind.

more by reference to the different frequencies with which certain types of offences are tried in the Crown Courts in the two cities[15] than to any fundamental differences of response by juries to these kinds of offences.

It is worth examining in relation to the London cases the possibilities of acquittal in complex fraud trials. It is very interesting that there was not a single fraud trial in the London sample which lasted as long as seven days and most of those that took over three days resulted in convictions. As was noted in relation to the Birmingham sample, it appears that the problem of juries perversely acquitting defendants in complex fraud cases is more often assumed than real. One explanation for the small number of such cases being contested has been stated in a leader in *The Times*, 11 January 1973, where it was argued that:

... guilty pleas to relatively minor [fraud] charges have been accepted in preference to running the considerable risk that more serious charges, if pursued before a jury, might result in perverse acquittals because jurors were unable to comprehend the evidence.

Although evidence for this argument from our own research is limited, there is some support for it from a number of sources. Again it illustrates the importance of examining the outcomes of jury cases in the wider context of decisions that are taken at earlier stages of the criminal process. Clearly, if individuals take decisions which represent accommodations to their assumed fears of jury perversity, this will have a critical bearing on such matters as the levels of acquittal. There is some evidence from our inquiry which suggests that the prosecution do indeed attempt in many cases to circumvent the jury in this way, though often the overriding consideration is not the fear of a perverse acquittal so much as the savings of time and cost that a guilty plea can produce.[16] One police officer in the sample who led an enormously complex fraud inquiry, conducted on an international scale, made a number of telling observations on the subject:

[15] See above Table 4 at p. 43.
[16] We have argued elsewhere that the saving of costs is very often a dominant consideration in the administration of justice: Baldwin and McConville (1977a) at pp. 106–9.

Case 113 (London) Sometimes the prosecution are prepared to accept a plea on lesser counts and sometimes the indictments are geared in such a way that we get a plea to something lesser but it's still a substantial plea. We gain a conviction at less cost to the country. In this case, it was obviously the court's wish that [the defendant] went away and saw the light of day [i.e. to plead guilty] because the evidence was overwhelming. It was going to cost a fortune to bring in the witnesses from all over the world. We'd been all over the world for months and months doing this investigation and it was so thorough that the man should have taken his counsel's advice to plead guilty. Finally, he succumbed to the advice of his counsel and pleaded guilty. I'm sure the fact that he succumbed reduced his sentence because he had saved so much public money.

A related problem is that of long trials[17] and it is worth examining the evidence in Birmingham and London on the question. The first, and obvious, point to make is that very long trials are exceptionally rare. Indeed, most contested trials, both in Birmingham and in London, were concluded within two days. The great bulk of cases which are tried by jury involve relatively simple, clear-cut questions, though the offences being tried may nevertheless be extremely serious. Only seven trials in the Birmingham Crown Court lasted over seven days, whereas eighteen in London took at least this long. We do not know whether the juries were confused by the complexities of the evidence in these long trials but we can say that the great majority (five in Birmingham and fourteen in London) resulted in the conviction of the defendants concerned. Nor did we find that any of these defendants fell within our category of questionable convictions (the subject dealt with in Chapter 5). In relation to both complex fraud cases and lengthy trials, fears that juries are commonly confused by the evidence seem to be exaggerated. In any event, such cases cannot explain why so high a proportion of acquittals by juries in the present samples were regarded by respondents as questionable.

[17] The leader in *The Times*, 11 January 1973, again makes a relevant point: 'One point of view is that it is unfair on jurors to keep them away from their ordinary work and other activities for months on end . . . it is a price which must be paid in the interests of justice. It is also said that a trial's extreme length makes it very difficult for members of a jury to assess properly and sift the evidence before them, and arrive at a balanced verdict. But there is no reason to think that this is in fact so. What indications there are . . . suggest that a jury is perfectly capable of coping adequately with a long trial.'

We have discussed throughout this chapter the extent to which respondents' opinions differed from those of the jury in cases resulting in acquittals. We have noted that the proportion of acquittals respondents regarded as doubtful was considerably higher than that identified by other researchers both in England and in the United States. It is appropriate to re-emphasize the point that, in a majority of trials that ended in acquittals, there was no real disagreement from most parties with the juries' verdicts. For most acquittals there was some readily identifiable factor, particularly a weakness in the prosecution case (for instance, the failure of a key witness to come up to proof on the day of the trial) or a reasonably convincing explanation offered by the defendant, which respondents acknowledged as justification for the verdict. Indeed, perhaps one of the most surprising findings is that, where the police are concerned, most acquittals are not seriously questioned. We drew attention in Chapter 3 to the ability of most police officers we interviewed (and indeed other respondents) to discriminate carefully between a general view they might hold of the jury system and a specific opinion about the outcome of a particular trial. It is true to say that we rarely encountered a respondent (other than perhaps certain defendants) who expressed strong disagreement with any verdict but who was not able to provide careful reasons for this view. This was particularly evident in the case of police officers, since we were able in lengthy interviews to probe deeply where we thought an answer unhelpful or superficial. In our judgment, no more than a handful of officers expressed doubts that they could not carefully elaborate and defend.

These considerations notwithstanding, the extent to which respondents, particularly in Birmingham, expressed strong criticisms of cases in which the jury acquitted is remarkable. We did not in any way expect it from the wealth of writing on the subject, nor could the questions that we were allowed to put to respondents have artificially stimulated criticism of the jury. It is a matter of judgment whether the proportion of acquittals is too high or too low; there is no proper rate for the job.[18] But the

[18] Some regard the matter in more clear-cut terms. Thus, Lord Devlin (1960) writes: 'If the success of a system of criminal prosecution is to be measured by the proportion of criminals whom it convicts and punishes, the English system must be regarded as a failure. Far too many people who have in fact committed crimes escape punishment.' (p. 113.)

number of defendants who seemed to us to have been acquitted in questionable circumstances, without any apparent equitable justification save in a handful of cases, suggests that trial by jury is a relatively crude instrument for establishing the truth. Moreover, we believe that the results of the following chapter, which deals with the smaller number of questionable convictions, give rise to much more serious doubts in this respect.

5

DOUBTFUL CONVICTIONS BY JURY

ALTHOUGH it is now well established that the verdict of a jury occasionally results in an unjust conviction, proving that a miscarriage of justice has occurred is a very difficult undertaking. Much of the evidence on wrongful convictions has been obtained only after long and detailed investigation of individual cases and many such examinations, whilst casting grave doubts upon the guilt of the accused, have been unable to demonstrate that there was a miscarriage of justice. For obvious reasons, this is not a subject that readily lends itself to empirical inquiry and only one systematic study of the phenomenon has been conducted—that by Brandon and Davies (1973) into cases of wrongful imprisonment.[1] Confining themselves to cases in which it had been officially acknowledged that an accused had been convicted of a crime he did not in fact commit and in which a prison sentence resulted, the authors identified seventy cases of wrongful imprisonment in England and Wales in the period 1950–70. This figure is of course an absolutely minute proportion of those convicted and sentenced to imprisonment during this perio but Brandon and Davies were of the view that it merely represented 'the tip of a much larger iceberg'. The hurdles to be overcome in order to establish innocence[2] may be thought in themselves to offer some justification for this pessimistic view.

Despite the existence of this problem, however, the interest shown by researchers in convictions by jury has been negligible. Although research in America has involved an examination of convictions, almost all researchers in England who have

[1] Numerous books have been written over the years about the cases of individuals who have been the victims of miscarriages of justice. Some writers have compiled descriptions of several such cases: see, for example, Frank and Frank (1957) and Borchard (1970).

[2] Brandon and Davies (1973) cite at p. 277 the following pertinent comment of Tom Sargant, Secretary of Justice: 'Whereas the judicial consideration of the results of an investigation could lead the court to the view that no jury would have convicted with all the facts before it, this is not the case once an appeal has been dismissed. Thereafter, absolute proof of innocence is required.'

looked at jury trials have restricted themselves to those cases that end as acquittals. As we have seen, the explanation for this approach in England has been a response to the fears that have been voiced about the proportion of allegedly guilty men able to secure acquittals before juries. Even so, the lack of attention given to conviction by jury is hard to understand because the conviction of the innocent represents a greater affront to justice than the acquittal of the guilty. Moreover, apart from the well-established fact that convictions are sometimes wrongful, the substance of the debate over jury equity contains what must be regarded as a tacit acceptance of the possibility of improper conviction. Those who approvingly admit sentiment or sympathy as factors which might properly influence juries must also recognize the possibility that convictions may on occasion spring from prejudice. If it is the case that juries sometimes wrongfully acquit through ignorance, misunderstanding, or sheer bad judgment, then it follows that they may in other cases improperly convict on the same basis. This is not to say that the incidence of wrongful conviction will be as high as that of acquittals against the evidence. On the contrary, there are numerous safeguards which are likely to make wrongful convictions much less common than perverse acquittals. These safeguards include the rules governing the interrogation of suspects, the exclusionary rules of evidence, the requirements for corroboration, and the high burden of proof on the prosecution in criminal trials. Nevertheless, safeguards of this kind do not always prevent the conviction of innocent men.

Having said this, it is important to emphasize that, in the discussion that follows, we cannot for fairly obvious reasons talk in terms of innocent men being found guilty. Although we believe that there is strong evidence from our inquiry that some defendants convicted by jury may have been innocent, we are not in a position to say that they in fact were so. It would require prolonged and painstaking investigation of individual cases to make confident statements about guilt or innocence and we cannot claim to have carried out such an inquiry. Our interest in this chapter lies with those cases in which a defendant has been found guilty by the jury and in which considerable doubts about the conviction have been raised by respondents. In other words, our concern is not primarily with the conviction of the innocent but with the possibility that the verdict of guilty was not justified.

Looking at the opinions expressed by respondents about jury convictions as a whole, it is apparent from Table 9 on page 51 that there was general agreement with the jury's verdict in the vast majority (88·4 per cent) of cases. It is most important to bear this fact in mind throughout the ensuing discussion which focuses on the small minority of cases about which doubts of varying kinds were voiced by respondents. We regard the results from this part of our inquiry as disquieting but we do not wish in any way to exaggerate the problems that we identify. We have attempted to exercise caution in classifying convictions as questionable. To take one example: if a respondent expressed himself uncertain of the outcome at the time of a jury's retirement, we thought this an insubstantial basis on which to doubt the conviction, and consequently classified the response as one in which the verdict was not questioned. As already noted, a similar rule was adopted in those cases in which respondents expected a verdict to be an acquittal. A conviction was classified as doubted only when a respondent made an explicit and unambiguous statement which appeared to us to raise serious doubts about the verdict in question. As was the case with the questionable acquittals discussed in Chapter 4, it is simply not possible to arrive at clear-cut or watertight categories and we see our analysis more as raising certain critical questions about present procedures than as offering definitive judgments.

We have adopted a somewhat different standard in classifying convictions as doubtful from that used in relation to acquittals in Chapter 4. Since an accused is entitled to an acquittal if he raises a reasonable doubt, we thought it appropriate to concentrate here on those cases in the Birmingham sample in which two or more respondents doubted a conviction. This produced a total of fifteen defendants, involved in fifteen separate trials (see Table 9 on page 51). The weight that we attach, therefore, to the opinions of the various parties involved in each trial differs from the weight we gave them in Chapter 4. Thus, for example, when a police officer expressed doubts after trial about the conviction of any individual, this raised in our minds greater misgivings about the verdict than if he voiced comparable doubts about cases that resulted in acquittals. It is important to note that, of the fifteen convictions classified as questionable, no fewer than thirteen were doubted by police officers. Of the other respondents, the judges expressed reservations about eight of the cases, the defence solicitors of twelve, and the prosecuting solicitors of seven. We would again emphasize that it is the extent to which the doubts of different groups of respondents coincide that is important here rather than the individual expressions of discontent. No such discrimination was possible in respect of London cases and these will be cited only for tentative comparison with Birmingham cases.

The result of adopting a working definition based upon at least two respondents independently stating their disquiet about a particular conviction is to exclude all cases in which only one respondent expressed concern, no matter how strongly that concern was felt. It also excludes those cases in which respondents felt that a conviction for a lesser offence than that returned by the jury would have been more appropriate. The following are a few examples of the sorts of cases we have *excluded*:

Case 182 [A defendant with no previous convictions convicted of wounding with intent. All respondents expected a conviction of unlawful wounding, the alternative and less serious charge.]

Judge: The conviction for wounding with intent, though justified by the evidence, was perhaps a little surprising, in view of the fact that the defendant, a pleasant young man, had been seriously provoked—and perhaps even attacked—by his victim. The jury, however, applied the letter of the law.

Police: There was enough evidence to convict him of unlawful wounding and it was purely circumstantial whether he intended to wound or whether it just occurred. Having committed him for trial on a charge of wounding with intent, I suppose I should have expected a conviction on that, but having listened to all the evidence I thought he would be convicted of unlawful wounding. I was a bit shocked in a way that he was convicted of the more serious charge. I don't think he would have been sent to prison if he had pleaded guilty to unlawful wounding. This was probably a defence failing—not pleading guilty to the lesser charge.

Case 198 [A charge of robbery which depended to a large extent on identification. The defendant's appeal was abandoned.]

Defence solicitor: This was an unusual case in which the prosecution evidence was not strong and the defendant gave good evidence. The judge's summing-up was such as to raise serious misgivings and this will in effect become the major ground of the appeal.

Case 340 [A charge of rape resulting in a sentence of three and a half years' imprisonment. The issue was consent.]
Defence solicitor: Even though the prosecution witnesses appeared to be consistent, I have grave doubts as to the defendant's guilt.
Police: The complainant and two other witnesses for the prosecution were very good witnesses. The defendant himself was very good in the box but I don't think the judge or the jury believed his story. I was surprised the judge was so hard on him [in his sentence] as the judge said that he was not particularly impressed with the complainant, obviously a person of somewhat loose morals. I did expect a conviction, however.

Another consequence of adopting a strict definition of questionable conviction is to exclude those cases in which a defendant may have been prejudiced by the judge's handling of the trial in court. If, for example, the defendant is convicted after an adverse summing-up, it is not likely that anyone, other than the defence, will question the verdict unless there are additional grounds for doing so. This point can be illustrated by considering the only two cases in the Birmingham sample in which leave to appeal against conviction was granted. In both cases, the defence solicitors were critical of the judge's handling of the trial and the prosecuting solicitor also commented upon alleged deficiencies in the summing-up. Since no respondent except the defence solicitor raised doubts about the verdicts returned, these cases were not included within our questionable conviction group. Yet in both cases the misgivings of the defence solicitors turned out to be well founded, the Court of Appeal quashing both convictions on appeal. The views of the respondents on these cases are reproduced below:

Case 92 [A charge of theft in which the defendant denied any involvement in the alleged offence]
Defence solicitor: Quite honestly, in legal terms the summing-up was wholly wrong. It was such that the judge said: 'Well, the prosecution witness did not identify the defendant but nevertheless he was the man who took the money.'
Prosecuting solicitor: The summing-up was over weighted in favour

of the prosecution. Although there was a misdirection in the summing-up, the total picture was too obvious for an acquittal.

Case 94 [A charge of theft in which the defence was alibi]
Defence solicitor: The accused made no written statement. The strength of the prosecution case mainly rested on verbal admissions to police officers which were disputed by the defendant. The judge summed-up against the defendant in an adverse manner, and contrary to the evidence called.
Prosecuting solicitor: The summing-up was weighted in favour of the prosecution. The general picture of the case provided a need for an answer. The only answer was theft by the accused.

It is arguable, therefore, that the definition of questionable convictions we have used is likely to understate the extent of the problem. This may well be so, since our classification of such cases depends upon individuals making explicit any doubts they might entertain, and the volunteering of such information depends on a number of uncontrollable factors. In addition to this, we have drawn our categories without regard to the defendants' views. This latter decision was taken with certain misgivings, because a small number of the defendants who protested their innocence in interviews made profound impressions upon us. We thought it right, however, to proceed with caution and to avoid any tendency to overstat the problem. We were successful in interviewing thirteen of these defendants and all claimed to have been innocent of the charges they faced. In London, we had to rely exclusively on the views of police officers about all cases and, on this basis alone, ten doubtful convictions in separate trials in London were identified.

Close observers of the English trial system agree that certain sorts of case and particular forms of evidence raise greater difficulties for juries, and more serious risks to defendants, than others. For instance, if a defendant is tried jointly with others, there is an increased likelihood that the additional complexities of the case will confuse a jury or that they may be prejudiced against the defendant merely because of his association with others whom they are satisfied are guilty. Other dangers include verbal confessions, identification evidence, and perjured testimony of witnesses. These well-known hazards have led the courts to develop rules of practice and procedure designed to minimize the risks to innocent defendants. Thus, for example, no statement by an accused person is admissible in evidence against him unless it is voluntary in the sense that it has not been obtained from him by fear of prejudice or hope of advantage held out by a person in authority or by oppression.[3] Moreover, even a voluntary statement may be ruled inadmissible if it was obtained in breach of the rules laid down to guide police interrogations of suspects.[4] It can be argued, of course, that the courts have not done enough to overcome these problems, and the recent study of Brandon and Davies (1973) identified many of the matters mentioned above as among the most frequent causes of wrongful imprisonment. They write:

Patterns which emerged frequently . . . were: unsatisfactory identification, particularly by confrontation between the accused and the witness; confessions made by the feeble-minded and the inadequate; evidence favourable to the defence withheld by the prosecution; certain joint trials; perjury, especially in cases involving sexual or quasi-sexual offences; badly-conducted defence; criminals as witnesses. (p. 21.)

This conclusion is in line with a report of Justice (1968), and it is worth while examining whether any of the hazards that have been identified were present in the group of questionable convictions in the Birmingham sample.

It came as something of a surprise to note that such factors seemed rarely relevant as causes of possibly wrongful conviction in this sample. On occasions, respondents mentioned some of these matters but, even then, they stressed that their effect was outweighed by other considerations. Thus, although five of the defendants in question had been involved with others in joint trials, in only one case, cited below, did any respondent feel that the defendant may have been prejudiced by being tried with others:

Case 226 [A case involving two charges of violence]
Defence solicitor: The accused was properly acquitted on count 1, and convicted, in our view wrongly, on count 2. There were two

[3] *Prager* [1972] 1 All E.R. 1114.

[4] These rules, known as the Judges' Rules, seek to regulate police conduct in interrogating suspects. They do not have the force of law though the trial judge may, in his discretion, exclude evidence which has been obtained in breach of them. We have elsewhere expressed our doubts about the extent to which the Judges' Rules operate as an effective check in practice on police excesses in this regard: see Baldwin and McConville (1977a) pp. 102–5.

other persons involved; one was acquitted of both charges and the other had left the country [before trial]. The jury possibly thought they had to convict someone.

There was one other case in which the possibility of guilt by association was mentioned but that was stated to be a subsidiary influence upon the course of the trial. Similarly, two cases turned largely upon identification evidence but in each instance respondents believed that evidence to be firm and reliable.

The possibility that there was perjured or mistaken testimony in some of these cases is more difficult to establish. It is undoubtedly true that the evidence of a number of witnesses in these cases was somewhat unsatisfactory but there is a great difference between evidence which is unsatisfactory through nervousness, memory lapse, or inadequate transmission and evidence which is fabricated. Most of the cases involved, in the view of the respondents, the former rather than the latter. There was only one possible exception, *case 291*, a case of violence in which the judge said that 'the prosecution left many loose ends untied'. The victims had previous convictions and the defendant had none, and the police officer observed:

I felt that the defendant had a rough deal. The case brought out the fact that he had no previous convictions, whereas the complainants had. In fact, I had arrested one of the complainants the previous year; they are all well-known trouble-makers. I felt the defendant had a rotten deal.

A more delicate problem which arises is that of verbal statements of admission alleged to have been made while the accused was under interrogation by the police. It is right to state that we ourselves feel considerable unease over the question of the interrogation of suspects by the police and particularly over what have become known as 'police verbals'.[5] There is no question whatever that police officers do on occasions attribute to a defendant a statement of admission that he did not in fact make. In the course of our research, we interviewed over 700 police officers and several privately admitted that this

[5] Police 'verbals' consist of the attribution to a defendant of a verbal admission to the offence charged. Our misgivings about this subject are discussed in Baldwin and McConville (1977a) at pp. 68–70.

is practised from time to time. We expected that the issue of the authenticity of oral admissions would be raised amongst the questionable conviction cases but we found little evidence of it. Indeed, in only three of the fifteen cases did the prosecution evidence include any kind of verbal admission by the defendant—a remarkably low proportion and much lower than the proportion for other cases in the whole sample. In two of these cases, the defence solicitor made the point that 'verbals' were virtually insurmountable without good, reliable evidence to counteract them. The defendants involved in both these cases complained bitterly about 'verbals' when we interviewed them after the trial. We shall never know the truth about these complaints but it is apparent that, the resentment of defendants notwithstanding, there was little evidence to suggest that verbal evidence played more than a minor part in the questionable convictions in this sample.

When we examined the views of respondents about these cases, we found that the sort of factors traditionally assumed to give rise to miscarriages of justice could not adequately explain them. We came to regard two other factors as being much more important: *first*, that the jury appeared in many of these cases to be too easily satisfied of the defendants' guilt because they failed to appreciate the high standard of proof required in criminal cases; *second*, that the jury apparently convicted the defendant through lack of comprehension of the issues involved. It is important to examine the cases which might be explained in these ways.

The standard of proof in criminal cases—proof beyond reasonable doubt—has long been a source of controversy among practising lawyers and legal commentators. Whereas in a civil case a simple balance of probability may constitute sufficient ground for a verdict, the accused in criminal cases is not to be convicted unless the jury is satisfied of his guilt beyond reasonable doubt. The higher standard of proof is applicable in criminal cases because of the principle that it is better to acquit some who are probably guilty than it is to convict any who are possibly innocent. The evidence from several pieces of research suggests, however, that jurors may not always apply the standard of proof in the way lawyers expect. In Simon and Mahan's (1971) study, for instance, it was found that jurors applied a less stringent interpretation of 'beyond reasonable doubt' than judges; in other words, jurors were more easily satisfied of the defendant's guilt.[6] In England, Sealy and Cornish (1973b) found that altering the instruction on the standard of proof did not produce in mock juries the kind of variation that lawyers suppose will follow, and concluded that their results showed 'how sceptical one may be of proposals for reform which depend for their effect upon an instruction that can be appreciated only by those who have training or experience enough to do so' (p. 222). There is some support for this position in the views of our respondents. One defence solicitor questioned whether the jury appreciated the subtleties of what was meant by a reasonable doubt, and in other cases respondents were of the view that there had been at least a reasonable doubt.[7] A few examples will illustrate the sorts of opinion expressed:

Case 108 [A man with no previous convictions charged with a motoring offence]
Defence solicitor: It was felt by the prosecution along with the defence that the defendant would be acquitted. The good impression given by the defence witness was enough in the defence's mind to ensure an acquittal.
Police Officer: I was a little surprised he was convicted. His witness I thought was quite convincing. On the basis of the evidence and the relevant law I would have anticipated that he would have been given the benefit of the doubt and therefore found not guilty.

Case 171 [A case in which the accused was of previous good character]
Judge: In this case, which was one of robbery, both victim and defendant were Indians. The evidence of the victim had to be given through interpreters. There were many minor inaccuracies and I was surprised that the jury felt able to rely to the extent they did on his evidence.

[6] See also on this question, Hoffman and Brodley (1952); Arens, Granfield and Susman (1965); Simon (1970); McCabe and Purves (1974); and Barber and Gordon (1976) especially at pp. 22–4, 76–80.

[7] McBarnet (1976) states well the difficulties involved in the legal requirement as to proof. She writes: 'There is no place in strict legal categories for the ambiguities which dog real life . . . Conviction . . . depends on a legal concept of proof, not on common-sense or scientific criteria which might well conclude the truth to be unknowable, not just in a philosophical sense but because of the circumstances and methods involved . . . The verdict is . . . a compoundly subjective construction of reality after the event—yet it is also a clearcut decision that the offence and the offender have or have not been proved beyond reasonable doubt. It is unambiguously black or white.' (pp. 173–4.)

Police: Apart from other weaknesses of the prosecution evidence, our witness was not too reliable. Right from the beginning the complainant seemed unreliable and we weren't entirely satisfied on the complaint that he was making.

Case 257 (London) [A retrial of a handling case]
Police: I wouldn't have been surprised if they had acquitted him. His story was more than plausible and he was very good in evidence. Our case was quite weak and I was surprised at the verdict. I have been generally satisfied with the jury but not on this occasion.

Case 396 (London) [A case of snatching a handbag]
Police: It was virtually my evidence—which was not very strong—against his and he was very plausible. He didn't dispute my story basically, he agreed with what I said. I don't know how they convicted really. On the evidence he was entitled to an acquittal; there was more than a doubt about it even in my mind.

These examples raise at least a possibility that in certain cases juries may be too easily convinced of a defendant's guilt. This is not to say, of course, that juries are in general insufficiently stringent in their interpretation of the standard of proof in criminal trials. Indeed, the instances of questionable acquittal discussed in Chapter 4 might be taken to belie this. The probable explanation is that the legal standard is a difficult, if not impossible, one for laymen to apply and that different juries interpret the standard in different ways.

For some cases, a less charitable explanation was suggested by respondents: that the jury convicted a defendant through stupidity or a lack of understanding of the issues involved. Perhaps the best illustration of this occurs in those cases in which the judge has given a strong summing-up on the evidence. Although a judge must not sum up in such a manner as to lead the jury to believe that he is directing them that they must find the facts in a particular way, there is no doubting the influence that a summing-up may have on the jury. Indeed, one piece of research concluded that much of the jury's deliberations was actually taken up with seeking to discover what was in the judge's mind and with trying to produce a verdict with which the judge would agree.[8] It is equally true that in some

[8] Bankowski and Mungham (1976) at p. 211 *et seq*. Other writers have drawn attention to the pre-eminent role of the judge in the English trial system: see especially Napley (1966); Griew (1967); and McCabe and Purves (1974).

cases a judge will take great care to ensure that the jury should not find a man guilty whom he believes to be innocent.[9] It was clear in a few cases, however, that despite great judicial care the jury nevertheless convicted:

Case 185 [A charge of going equipped for theft, for a conviction on which it must be proved that the defendant intended to use the article—in this case a screwdriver—in the course of, or in connection with, any burglary, theft or cheat.]

Judge: In this case, the jury after retiring sent a note that they had reached a majority verdict 'on intent'. They were told that they must be unanimous. They returned and the foreman said 'guilty with intent'. I did not accept this and the foreman then said they were satisfied that the defendant intended to steal but saw no point in him using the articles listed in the charge for any theft. They were then directed that if the defendant did not intend to use the articles for theft, he could not be said to have them in his possession in connection with theft and they *must* acquit—they then CONVICTED! [Judge's own emphasis.]

Case 380 [A serious case of violence in which leave to appeal against conviction was refused]

Judge: The Crown case was not strong. The jury were strongly directed that they should only draw the inference that the defendant had something to hide from his lies to the police if they were *forced* to do so—they were prepared to draw that inference.

Defence solicitor: This was a very unsatisfactory case. There is bound to be an appeal. A majority verdict after six hours' deliberation by the jury over less than two days' evidence!

Case 402 [A charge of handling stolen goods]

Judge: This was a case which could have gone either way. It was not a particularly strong case for the prosecution. I for my part would have acquitted, but it was perfectly open to the jury to decide as they did.

Defence solicitor: Idiotic jury didn't do what the judge directed. The summing-up indicated that the prosecution had not proved the essential element of knowledge. The judge expressed his view of the decision by a conditional discharge.

Police: I was expecting a not guilty verdict. The judge in his

---

[9] Fry (1921) quotes Lord Justice Fry as saying: 'Some judges almost tell a jury how they ought to find and so seem to me to assume a function which is not theirs according to our constitution. I have always striven to avoid doing this, and to leave the question really as well as formally to the jury, taking, however, great care that they should never find a man guilty whom I believed innocent.' (p. 69).

summing-up more or less said that guilty knowledge hadn't been proved.

It seems possible, therefore, that in some cases the jury failed through ignorance, confusion, or stupidity to pick up cues from the judge's summing-up.[10] In cases in this category, there is one sensitive question which must be raised and this concerns the possibility that in some of these cases the jury might have been prejudiced against the defendant on racial grounds. This was in fact a possibility identified by Kalven and Zeisel (1966) and by other collaborators in the Chicago Jury Project.[11] Kalven and Zeisel produced evidence that members of certain minority groups were sometimes regarded as 'unattractive' by juries and this factor served to reduce their credibility in the eyes of the jury. Furthermore, Cornish (1968) reported that the jurors he had interviewed generally appeared to have leaned over backwards to be fair in cases in which there had been black defendants, but continued: 'none of them had been concerned with cases which are most likely to raise deep prejudice, such as homicide, sexual assault or some form of mob violence' (p. 141). He pointed out that, since such cases occur from time to time, a study should be made to discover whether racial prejudice leads juries to reach unjustifiable verdicts, especially of guilt in criminal cases. The information that we have on this question is no substitute for the sort of detailed study Cornish had in mind but it does support his view that some inquiry would be valuable. We shall return to this question in Chapter 8 but it is appropriate to discuss some relevant matters at this point.

In the course of our interviews with police officers in Birmingham, our attention was occasionally drawn to what they saw as racial prejudice on the part of the jury. One officer remarked, for instance, that a West Indian defendant, whom he acknowledged had probably been wrongly charged, was none the less fortunate to have gained an acquittal in the face of

---

[10] In *case 27*, the defence solicitor said: 'Another matter which troubles me a little—the jury returned to ask a question. Neither the question nor the answer to it could have had the slightest bearing on the verdict. Within seconds of receiving the answer to that question, they arrived at a unanimous verdict of "guilty". What on earth had they been discussing? Surely not the evidence!'

[11] See Kalven and Zeisel (1966) at p. 210 *et seq*, and Broeder (1965a and 1966).

possible prejudice. In a case which we classified as a doubtful conviction, the issue was raised explicitly on a charge of rape. The judge had summed up in favour of an acquittal and the prosecuting solicitor thought the evidence too weak for the jury to find the defendant guilty. The police officer's view on the outcome is set out below:

Case 74 [A case of rape alleged to have been committed by a West Indian]

Police Officer: It was pretty obvious, and we had all virtually agreed, that there were so many lies, you couldn't find him guilty. Normally, if there are lies floating around, the defendant should get the benefit. All the way through I was expecting an acquittal. I was most surprised when the jury came back. I do not believe [the victim], I never believed her for one moment. The coloured men that were interviewed by us [the witnesses for the defence], I interviewed them all personally and I believed them. The judge really summed up for a not guilty verdict. The defendant initially told us a lie but so did [the victim]. This was brought out at the trial, that she had lied and they still found him guilty. I don't think the jury believed the defendant because he was coloured. The defence witnesses were very good; I believed them. I think it was a failure on the part of the jury to believe them because they were coloured.

The expression of such views does not by any means establish that juries are moved by racial prejudice but there is other evidence which is at least suggestive. Within the group of doubtful conviction cases, no fewer than eight out of fifteen involved black defendants, whereas there were only seven such defendants out of the 41 cases in the questionable acquittal group discussed in Chapter 4. Too much should not be made of this, however, since the figures are too small to allow meaningful generalizations to be made and, overall, the proportion of black defendants appearing before juries in Birmingham was almost a third. But the figures do suggest that the possibility of racial prejudice by some juries is one that deserves serious attention, the more so since six of the eight black defendants were charged with those offences (violence and sexual assault) identified by Cornish as most likely to give rise to strong antipathy and prejudice.

It is important at this point to provide some details of the sort of cases involved in this group of questionable convictions in Birmingham. Although seven of the defendants admitted that they had committed the act alleged (e.g. striking the victim), their defence being that they lacked the necessary guilty mind, it is interesting that in the cases of the other eight defendants, the defence was a complete denial of any involvement whatever in the offences charged. As to the charges themselves, it is clear that a majority of them were serious cases. There were two murder cases, a rape, and three other offences involving violence. The remainder consisted of a miscellaneous collection of offences, including six against property, of varying degrees of seriousness. A further indication of the gravity of the charges is provided by the fact that nine defendants were sentenced to a term of imprisonment (in five cases, the term exceeded three years), one received a suspended prison sentence, four were fined, and one was given a conditional discharge. The sentences meted out to these defendants raise an apparent contradiction, since, when the trial judge expressed doubts about the verdict, one might have expected these doubts to be reflected in the passing of lenient sentences. Given the virtually unfettered discretion in sentencing that judges exercise, one can never be sure that the trial judge did not in fact do this. Indeed, in a majority of those cases in which the judge himself questioned the conviction, the sentences seemed to us, if anything, lenient. In any event, it seems likely that judges would generally feel constrained to give effect to the verdict of the jury rather than to their own private opinions.

Not only were the cases serious, but the social consequences to the defendants concerned appeared, in many cases, quite shattering, not least because seven of them had no previous convictions and twelve had never before been to prison. The sapping effect that imprisonment may have on a defendant's morale and the disruption it causes to family relationships can be readily understood, but even when a custodial sentence is not imposed, the fact of conviction may have far-reaching and damaging consequences for a defendant.[12] In *case 65*, for example, where all the respondents raised doubts about the conviction and the defence solicitor described the verdict as 'per-

[12] See, for example, Morris (1965); Martin and Webster (1971); and Boshier and Johnson (1974).

verse', the defendant was fined and described the ways in which the conviction had affected him as follows:[13]

It has been all worry. I haven't eaten or slept for weeks. I was determined to stand up and be counted. I was offered a caution by the police if I admitted guilt to them. I refused to do this and now I have been penalized for my principles, for not taking the easy way out. I would have been promoted at work but for this trial amd I won't get another chance now. My financial position received a tremendous blow. The solicitor's bill alone cost over £300 and, if I appeal, a transcript will cost over £700 and the whole thing may be thousands. My health has suffered most. The strain brought on a mild heart attack and has left me agitated and depressed. I thought then, if I get off, I will sue them for every penny they've got for all the worry and misery its caused me and my wife. No one has the right to do that to anyone.

We can say of these convictions, then, that there was general and considerable disquiet amongst respondents about the juries' verdicts. They all raise important questions, particularly because the offences in question were often extremely serious and the consequences to the defendants concerned were in most cases severe. The stock answer to such worries is to draw attention to current appeals procedures, and most defendants at the time we interviewed them were actively considering with their legal advisers the possibility of an appeal. Sometimes the defence solicitor himself mentioned this in the questionnaire he completed for us. To our surprise, however, only three of the defendants in the end applied for leave to appeal. The reasons for the low level of appeals in respect of this group of questionable convictions deserve close examination. For whilst it is true that many defendants do not appeal because they have in fact committed the offence with which they were charged and, on conviction, give up the fight, the cases within our category of questionable convictions cannot in our judgment be explained in this way.

Generally speaking, there are several obstacles facing defendants who may wish to appeal against their conviction to the Court of Appeal. In the first place, the defendant may not be given adequate advice on appeal following the verdict. In

---

[13] All the facts relating to the offence mentioned by the defendant were confirmed independently by the police officer in charge of the case.

Zander's survey (1972), it was found that many defendants who had applied for leave to appeal had had no legal advice at all about it. Other defendants in his sample had been given no assistance with the drafting of their grounds for appeal and a few had even appealed against the advice of their barrister.[14] This survey eventually led to changes in the procedure for giving advice on appeal, though there was still some complaint from the defendants we interviewed that no such advice had been given.[15] Second, there is a formal deterrent to appeals which arises from an announcement in 1970 made by the then Lord Chief Justice.[16] In that announcement, the Lord Chief Justice pointed out that the number of applications for leave to appeal was rising rapidly and that the delays caused by this had become unacceptable. He indicated that 'unarguable' applications might in the future be punished by ordering that some of the time during which the prisoner is in custody after putting in his notice of application is not to count towards his sentence. This announcement had a speedy effect; the rate of applications for leave to appeal fell from about 12,000 to 6,000 a year. Thirdly, the level of success of appeals is so low that a conscious decision not to appeal is easily justified. In England and Wales in 1976, 6,201 defendants applied for leave to appeal to the Court of Appeal, of whom 1,526 appealed against conviction.[17] Most applications, however, were refused or abandoned. Indeed, of those appealing against conviction, only 396 were actually heard by the Court, the conviction being quashed in 145 cases. The findings of our research correspond to these national statistics. Of the 256 defendants convicted by jury in

---

[14] Even when counsel has advised that there are grounds for appeal, a defendant who is not privately represented may be at a considerable disadvantage. His application will normally be placed before a single judge who makes a decision without hearing oral argument. Privately represented applicants, who usually have their cases placed directly before the Court of Appeal (where the prospects of success are higher) have the benefit of having counsel appearing in person to reinforce his written opinion and deal with any points raised.

[15] The new procedure is designed to ensure that counsel's advice about appeal is in writing and that the solicitor communicates this opinion to the defendant: see Zander (1975). Some of the cases in our sample were deeply disturbing to us personally and, in the absence of any legal advice, we sometimes offered the defendants concerned the best advice we could in the circumstances.

[16] Practice Note [1970] 1 W.L.R. 663.

[17] Home Office, *Criminal Statistics: England and Wales 1976*, H.M.S.O. Cmnd 6909 at p. 330.

Birmingham, 42 applied for leave to appeal against conviction and leave to appeal was granted in only two cases.[18] In the two appeals heard, which were discussed earlier in this chapter, the Court of Appeal quashed both convictions.[19] In our group of questionable convictions, there were two applications for leave to appeal against conviction, both of which were refused.[20]

These considerations cannot, however, explain the low rate of appeal within the questionable conviction category because the defendant had often had the benefit of professional advice and the grievances were readily apparent. The problem, it seems, is more fundamental and raises, as we see it, a major objection to trial by jury. The basic difficulty can be stated shortly: the Court of Appeal is reluctant to interfere with a verdict of a jury unless it feels the jury was misled on a question of law or by some irregularity in the trial or misdirection of the judge. Thus, although the Court of Appeal now appears more willing to disturb the verdict of a jury,[21] it nevertheless remains the case that an innocent defendant who wishes to appeal is much better placed if he can point to some error of law or misdirection of the trial judge. As Williams (1963) put it, after reviewing appeal procedures: 'The upshot is that it is far easier for a person convicted by a jury to take and win an appeal on an unmeritorious point of procedure or evidence than it is for him to re-open on appeal the really serious question of his guilt.' (p. 331.)

As far as we could tell, it was this consideration that explained the very low level of appeals even in those cases regarded by respondents as doubtful. From the defendants' point of view, the pity was that there had not been, in any of the cases, a procedural irregularity or misdirection by the trial judge. On the contrary, respondents were quick to point out that the summing-up by the judge had as a rule been balanced and fair; indeed, in some instances it had been slanted in the

[18] We are indebted to Mr. A. F. P. Ottway of the Criminal Appeal Office for facilitating access to the information on the outcome of appeals.

[19] There were, in addition, 23 applications for leave to appeal against sentence, two of which were granted, the sentence being varied in both cases.

[20] There was also one application for leave to appeal against sentence which was refused.

[21] Following *Cooper* [1968] 3 W.L.R. 1225, where the Court of Appeal said that it would interfere if it had 'some lurking doubt' which caused it to wonder whether an injustice had occurred.

defendant's favour. In other words, there was no substantive point to take on appeal except a belief that the jury had come to a wrong conclusion on the evidence. It was this which caused one defence solicitor to comment: '. . . there should be a right of appeal against conviction by a jury even though there be no fault in summing-up and no additional evidence available, or misdirection by the judge.' These defendants were for the purposes of appeal at a disadvantage precisely because their trials had been conducted properly and fairly.[22]

In a real sense, therefore, it is this group of cases which raises the most difficult and fundamental questions about the efficacy of trial by jury. On the narrow classification adopted here, it appears that over 5 per cent of those found guilty by jury were convicted in questionable circumstances and were left, for all practical purposes, without effective remedy on appeal.[23] Moreover, the absence of a remedy in these cases is inseparably linked to the existence of trial by jury because appellate review is heavily circumscribed by the fact that the jury does not give reasons for its decisions. If the jury did convict through mis-understanding or from prejudice, the inscrutability of the ver-dict (which judges have over the years been careful to protect) ensures that this will remain concealed. If reasoned decisions were given, of course, the Court of Appeal would be much better placed to undertake a thorough review of the verdict but it would be foolish to imagine that the jury could ever be required to state its reasons for reaching a particular determi-nation. As Cornish (1968) has put it, the absence of reasons for its decision 'is surely a characteristic which is bound to last as long as the jury system itself—once the inscrutability principle has gone, the time has come to set up another kind of tribunal' (p. 258).

This inescapable conclusion has led some to argue for the abolition of trial by jury and its replacement by a professional tribunal which would give a reasoned judgment when it con-victed anybody of a criminal offence. However that may be, it is

---

[22] See, in this context, Brandon and Davies (1973) at pp. 110–11; Williams (1963) at p. 330.
[23] It is always open to a convicted person to petition the Home Office for a review of his case, and about 4,000 such petitions are made every year. The problems with this review procedure, which is very rarely successful, are discussed in the report by Justice (1968).

our contention that the questionable conviction of those charged with serious offences, resulting in devastating social consequences for the defendant and his family, in circumstances which effectively pre-empt any review, is sufficient to raise doubts about the very basis of trial by jury.

6

JURY COMPOSITION AND JURY VERDICTS

THE notion, to which many trial lawyers subscribe, that the composition of a particular jury is likely to have an important bearing on the verdict it returns, might be taken to represent a serious criticism of the institution. For if verdicts really are as strongly affected by the character of each jury as this implies, it is hard to defend a tribunal whose verdicts may be conditioned more by its membership than by the evidence given in the trial. Yet the emphasis upon the importance of hand-picking jurors and challenging those assumed to be unsympathetic to the prosecution or defence remains very much part of the conventional wisdom about juries. It is also commonly apparent even in the views of those whose praise of the system of jury trial is most generous.[1] This is a strange paradox and one not easily understood for it seems to conflict directly with the idea that trial by jury consists of trial by one's peers randomly selected from the community. Although this paradox may be little more than an indication of the disingenuousness that sometimes characterizes discussions of the subject of trial by jury, the relationship between the composition of the jury and the verdict it returns deserves close investigation because such evidence as there is suggests certain important correlations. The research on the subject is, it is true, contradictory in nature but there is some evidence to show that young people often are more sympathetic to the defence than are the old;[2] that manual workers' decisions frequently are at variance with those of white-collar workers;[3] and that women jurors sometimes

[1] Friloux (1975), an American lawyer, notes that: 'A competent trial lawyer realizes that many cases are literally won or lost at the very initial stage of a criminal trial: selecting the jury' (p. 220). Yet he argues later that: '. . . the resultant panel, with all its many variances, is still the most productive fact finding device yet developed in the Anglo-Saxon system and the American Criminal Justice system which evolved from it' (p. 224).
[2] See, particularly, Simon (1967); Sealy and Cornish (1973a); and Van Dyke (1977).
[3] See, for instance, Broeder (1965b); Hermann (1970); Adler (1973); Sealy and Cornish (1973a); and Van Dyke (1977).

determine cases differently from men.[4] Most of this evidence, however, has been drawn from research concerned with the deliberations of simulated juries and, for the reasons given in Chapter 1, provides a shaky basis on which to develop generalizations about the behaviour of real juries. Moreover, these findings are not supported by the observations of lawyers involved in those trials in the United States where sophisticated social science techniques have been employed to aid the selection of jurors likely to be predisposed towards the defence. The failure of these techniques in several trials to produce the verdict desired has served to demonstrate the difficulty of predicting how the particular social mix that comprises any jury will operate in practice.[5] Indeed, it would seem that these elaborate 'scientific' approaches to jury selection have proved little more effective in producing a desired result than the hunch and guesswork of trial lawyers.

We attached great importance to examining the relationship between the composition of the jury and the verdict it returned. Although we were unable to investigate the composition of juries in the London sample, we were extremely fortunate to have had the co-operation of the Crown Court authorities in Birmingham who, throughout the course of our research, completed for every trial in which a jury was empanelled a standardized form on jury composition. On this form, details were recorded of each juror's name, sex, age, occupation, race, and the number of times he had previously sat on a jury.[6] We understand that such information on jurors has never before been released to researchers in England, and we believe that it has only rarely been made available in the United States. Indeed, some of the detailed information that we were given is not even available to counsel at the time of the trial. For example, following a directive issued by the Lord Chancellor in August 1973, jury lists can no longer include the occupations of

---

[4] There is a good deal of inconsistency on this point: see, for instance, Miller (1922); Weld and Danzig (1940); Snyder (1971); Nagel and Weitzman (1972); Sealy and Cornish (1973a); and Van Dyke (1977).

[5] Interesting discussions of the phenomenon of 'scientific' jury selection are given in Schulman *et al.* (1973); Saks (1976); and Van Dyke (1977).

[6] We acknowledge the help given in the collection of this information by officials of the Lord Chancellor's Department at the Crown Court centre at Birmingham. We are particularly indebted to the Court's chief clerk, Mr. S. Carlton.

those on the jury panel.[7] With the information we were given, we were able to examine two specific questions that are central to any discussion of jury trial: first, how representative are jurors of the community at large? Second, what is the nature of the relationship between the socio-economic background of juries and the verdicts they return? In relation to the latter question, it seems that the exercise we were able to undertake using jurors from a substantial number of actual, not simulated, trials is the first that has been based on criminal trials.[8]

In England, unlike the United States, the way that jurors are selected is essentially very simple. Though there are certain variations of detail between different areas of the country, the basic procedures followed are the same. Names are selected from the electoral roll and individuals contacted by post some time before their service is due to start. A sizeable proportion of those contacted state that they are unable to sit and, if the reasons are deemed sufficiently pressing, they will as a rule be excused or at least have their term of service deferred. The practice adopted in Birmingham, and in other Crown Court centres, appears to be to grant excusals fairly readily, without rigorous inquiry into the strength or validity of the grounds that are put forward. The resulting jury pool may therefore be markedly different in terms of its social composition from that originally summoned for service.

In examining the backgrounds of jurors in the Birmingham Crown Court, useful comparisons can be made with material relating to the Birmingham populace as a whole. This material has been derived from two sources—the statistics compiled by the West Midlands County Council based on a 1 per cent household survey conducted in 1976, supplemented by the material available in the 1971 national census. The over-all comparison between this information and that relating to juries shows that juries in Birmingham in 1975 and 1976 were in

---

[7] Shortly after the Lord Chancellor's directive, the Bar Council issued a statement regretting this new practice: 'It is felt that the new directive will hamper both the prosecution and the defence, and it is not in the interests of the administration of justice.' (May 1974.)

[8] In the United States, some studies of civil juries have used real jurors: see, for example, Snyder (1971); Nagel and Weitzman (1972); and Adler (1973). In studies involving criminal trials, the number of jurors involved has invariably been very small: see Broeder (1965a; 1965b; 1965c).

important respects representative of the wider community but much less so in others. Juries can never be wholly representative since many groups are made specifically ineligible for service, but the objective of jury selection is to obtain a genuine social mix. That this is achieved in Birmingham, at least in some measure, nevertheless comes as something of a surprise since the available research evidence, derived exclusively from empirical studies of cities in the United States, has on the whole demonstrated how fundamentally unrepresentative of the wider community jurors tend to be.[9] The following passage of Van Dyke (1977), for example, which is based on demographic data collected on juries sitting throughout the United States, summarizes this position:

... in most courts in the United States significant segments of the population are still not included on juries as often as they would be in a completely random system aimed at impaneling a representative cross-section. Blue-collar workers, non-whites, the young, the elderly, and women are the groups most widely underrepresented on juries, and in many jurisdictions, the underrepresentation of these groups is substantial and dramatic. (p. 24.)

This social imbalance is sometimes assumed to be partly due to the number of challenges against individual jurors that can be made by both the defence and the prosecution, rather than because of any deficiencies in the selection procedures themselves. In America, much more than in England, there remains a possibility that such challenges will make some juries totally unrepresentative. There is in America an elaborate procedure (the *voir dire*) by means of which potential jurors can be questioned in court and removed from the jury pool if it seems that they are likely to be biased in the trial. In England, there is no equivalent procedure although the defence is allowed a certain number of peremptory challenges (i.e. without giving any reason for doing so)[10] and an unlimited number when a reason-

---

[9] See, on this, Robinson (1950); Mills (1962; 1969); Vanderzell (1966); Beiser (1973); Buckhout (1973); Carlson, Halper, and Whitcomb (1977); and Van Dyke (1977).

[10] At the time of the research, each defendant was allowed to exercise up to seven peremptory challenges. The number of such challenges that could be made in trials involving multiple defendants sometimes led to difficulties, and the Criminal Law Act, 1977, reduced each defendant's entitlement to three.

able cause is shown. Similarly, the prosecution may challenge for cause and, though it has no right of peremptory challenge as such, it may, without giving any reason, require a juror to 'stand by' whereupon that juror is excluded from the panel.[11] When the Morris Committee (1965) investigated the frequency of challenges, it was found that 'only in a relatively small minority of cases is any use made of the right of peremptory challenge'.[12] A survey carried out on the Committee's behalf in 1964 showed that, of 118 juries sworn at the Old Bailey, there was no peremptory challenge by the defence in 104, and in the other 14 cases, the defence challenged a total of only 26 jurors.[13] More recently, however, there has been growing concern that the exercise of the right of peremptory challenge, particularly in cases involving multiple defendants, has been abused by over-use. In the course of the debates in the House of Lords on the Criminal Law Act (1977), for example, a barrister admitted that he had himself abused the peremptory challenge when defending robbers, and continued:[14] 'There was absolutely no doubt that we could influence the composition of a jury if there were five or six robbers before a court by means of 35 challenges, so that we eventually got a layabout lot of unemployed males on the jury.' According to him, the practice was not confined to the defence, for he added: 'When appearing on behalf of the Crown I used to stand by jurors on behalf of the prosecution just as shamelessly.' Although these personal observations would suggest that challenges can have an important bearing upon jury composition, the results of our research in Birmingham tend by and large to tally with those of the Morris Committee. We found that the right of challenge was exercised in no more than one trial in seven, and only exceptionally was there more than a single challenge in a case. In the vast majority of cases, the challenge was exercised by the defence. Altogether only 101 challenges were made by the 370

[11] Unless there are insufficient persons remaining on the panel to make up a full jury.

[12] Morris Committee (1965) para. 327.

[13] Ibid. para. 325. Similar results were found in the other courts examined.

[14] The Earl of Mansfield, 386, *House of Lords (Debates)*, col. 461. Lord Hale agreed with these remarks: ibid. at col. 462. See, generally, 386, *House of Lords (Debates)*, cols. 458–65.

defendants who were tried by jury in Birmingham,[15] and as many as three-quarters of those who made such challenges were at the end of the day convicted.[16] It does not seem, therefore, that the opportunity to challenge jurors in these ways made much difference in Birmingham to the final composition of any jury and, where it was exercised, it proved to be an ineffective means of obtaining a noticeably sympathetic jury.[17]

In attempting to describe the social background of jurors, we have included all cases in which a jury was empanelled, regardless of whether the case ran its full course or not. This means that the juries who were sitting in the cases of those defendants acquitted on the direction of the judge, as well as those involved in cases where the defendants changed their plea to guilty after the trial had started, are included for this purpose. Table 2 on page 40 shows that in all 66 defendants were concerned in directed acquittals or in change of plea cases, though these in fact involved only 50 different juries. To have discussed the background of jurors simply in terms of those juries who decided the cases of the 370 defendants actually tried by jury would, in this instance, have distorted the picture. Altogether there were 326 different juries empanelled, and it is interesting to examine the extent to which the 3,912 individuals who made them up constituted a representative cross-section of the Birmingham populace as a whole. This can be done only in a relatively crude fashion,[18] though certain patterns emerge so

[15] A separate survey conducted by the Metropolitan Police Force suggests that the right of challenge is exercised much more frequently by defendants in London. In 341 trials heard in a two-month period in 1976 in the Old Bailey and Inner London Crown Court, almost one-third of defendants challenged members of the jury panel. When defendants made challenges, they challenged on average many more jurors than defendants did in Birmingham, and no fewer than 19 used their full quota of seven peremptory challenges. By comparison, very few jurors were asked by the prosecution to stand by. We are indebted to Commander G. B. Collins for supplying this information.

[16] No more than a handful of those who challenged jurors could be said to be dangerous or professional criminals.

[17] Cf. Judge E. Clarke (1975) at p. 48: 'Personally I believe that, except in very rare cases, challenging is a waste of time.'

[18] There are several important reasons for this. In the first place, jurors who sat on two or more different juries have been counted separately for each sitting. Though it would have distorted the over-all picture on jurors' backgrounds to have done otherwise, it means none the less that like is not strictly being compared with like. Secondly, there are numerous deficiencies in the census statistics themselves and it is well known that certain groups are heavily under-enumerated in any census. (See, on this point,

clearly that they cannot be explained away in terms of the limitations of the exercise itself.

The aim in selecting juries is to provide a tribunal that is both impartial and representative of the community at large. The Morris Committee (1965) rejected suggestions favouring the creation of expert juries either in general or for particularly difficult criminal cases.[19] The Committee's recommendations on jury service were based upon their assessment of the qualities which they thought were required of jurors:

> It is necessary to have on a jury men and women who will bring common sense to their task of exercising judgment; who have knowledge of the ways of the world and of the ways of human beings; who have a sense of belonging to a community; who are actuated by a desire to see fair play; and above all who strive to come to an honest conclusion in regard to the issues which are for them to decide. (para 53.)

The Committee took the view that all members of the community were capable of fulfilling these criteria and accordingly recommended abolition of the requirement that jurors be property owners or householders. They proposed that the basic requirement for jury service should be citizenship, as evidenced by inclusion in the electoral register. After years of debate and considerable stalling in official quarters, this recommendation was finally implemented in the Criminal Justice Act of 1972. It is interesting to see how far these changes have produced juries that, in the words of the Morris Committee, 'represent a cross-section drawn at random from the community'.

There can be little doubt that the widened enfranchisement has profoundly changed the character of juries trying cases in the Crown Court. The memorable phrase of Devlin (1956) that juries are 'predominantly male, middle-aged, middle-minded and middle-class' is no longer an accurate description of juries today. Jurors are now much less middle-class in character and much younger[20] than they used to be. Certainly by 1975 and

---

Rose *et al.* (1969) chapter 9). Finally, though we have been able to collect information on the challenges made against members of the jury pool, we know neither how many were excused jury service nor the numbers rendered ineligible for jury service because of the nature of their occupations (e.g. police officers, practising lawyers).

[19] See para. 343 of their report.

[20] The 1972 Act also reduced the age at which individuals become eligible for jury service from 21 to 18 and raised the upper age limit to 65.

1976, in Birmingham at least, the abolition of the property qualification had dramatically affected the composition of juries. At the time of our research, the juries in question had acquired a distinctly working-class character: indeed, a majority of jurors were manual workers, or the wives of manual workers.[21] It is, however, evident from Table 10 that, when the proportions of each occupational grouping are compared to those of the Census (using the Registrar General's classification[22]), manual workers, and particularly unskilled manual workers, are still somewhat under-represented on juries.

TABLE 10

The social class composition of jurors in Birmingham

Registrar General's classification		Jurors empanelled (1975 and 1976) (%)		Birmingham populace (1971 Census) (%)
Social Class I:	Professional occupations	143	3·9	2·5
Social Class II:	Intermediate occupations	461	12·6	12·0
Social Class III:	Skilled occupations (non-manual)	755	20·7	20·2
	Skilled occupations (manual)	1,393	38·1	30·6
Social Class IV:	Partly skilled occupations	777	21·3	25·9
Social Class V:	Unskilled	125	3·4	8·8
Not classifiable or not known		258	–	–
		3,912	100·0	100·0

Although the property qualification, which had existed unchanged from 1825, had, as one writer noted, 'quite rivalled

[21] This is in direct contrast to the results of studies concerned with the social background of the other main group of laymen used extensively in the English criminal justice system—lay magistrates. On this, see Hood (1972) chapter 3, and Baldwin (1976).

[22] It was not possible to use the more recent material derived from the 1976 survey of households in Birmingham for this purpose since, at the time of writing, the analysis of occupational data had not been carried out by the West Midlands County Council.

Charles II in unconscionable slowness of death',[23] the drastic change in the occupational background of jurors has nevertheless occurred very suddenly indeed. Part of the reason for the official resistance to this change—and resistance to the lowering of the age of eligibility for jury service —has without doubt been the fear of an increase in the numbers of wayward verdicts that such changes might bring about. We cannot say whether the number of such verdicts has increased since the change,[24] but we shall examine later in this chapter the extent to which differences in the social class composition of juries are related to the verdicts returned in the present sample.

The abolition of the property qualification and the lowering of the age of eligibility for jury service have also produced changes in the age structure of juries no less revolutionary than those noted in relation to social class. Overnight, the average age of jurors has very markedly fallen. If the figures for Birmingham set out in Table 11 are any guide, there is nowadays a much more even spread of age-groups represented on juries than at any time earlier.

TABLE 11

The ages of Birmingham jurors

	Jurors empanelled (1975 and 1976)		Birmingham populace (1976 survey)
		(%)	(%)
Under 21	202	5·2	7·5
21–9	845	21·7	21·4
30–9	718	18·5	19·5
40–9	863	22·2	20·3
50–9	960	24·7	19·8
60 or over	301	7·7	11·5
Not known	23	–	–
	3,912	100·0	100·0

[23] Cornish (1973) at p. 25.

[24] A study conducted by the Home Office Statistical Department (1975) has compared rates of acquittal in 1974 on a national basis for a three-month period after the changes in the qualifications for jury service with a three-month period prior to the revisions. No significant differences in over-all rates of acquittal were noted in the report as a result of the changes in the qualifications.

Tables 10 and 11 show, in terms of occupation and age, a remarkable congruence between those who sit on juries on the one hand and residents of Birmingham on the other. Though, for the reasons already stated, the comparisons are necessarily limited, there can be little doubt that juries are, in these two respects at least, reasonably representative of the population of Birmingham. In two other respects, however, the juries empanelled during 1975 and 1976 in Birmingham were not representative of the community at large.

The Morris Committee devoted considerable attention to the question of female representation on juries. The effect of the old requirement that a juror must in general be a householder was that women formed only 11 per cent of the total number of available jurors, and the Committee took the view that a system 'which has the effect of arbitrarily restricting the number of women jurors is indefensible'. It is perhaps surprising that, after the implementation of the Committee's recommendations, the most obvious discrepancy between the characteristics of jurors in Birmingham compared to those of the population of Birmingham as a whole relates to sex. In the period of our research, 72·5 per cent of jurors were male, a rather startling variation from the figure of 49·7 per cent males in the relevant age-groups given in the 1976 survey of households. Two factors probably account for this difference. First, more men than women are summoned for jury service in Birmingham[25] and, secondly, more women apply for, and are granted, excusals from jury service, particularly on the grounds of pressing family commitments.[26] It is these two factors which probably account for the considerable under-representation of females on Birmingham juries.

The second difference relates to race. For the years 1975 and 1976, there appeared to be a serious under-representation on Birmingham juries of those from the New Commonwealth

[25] The unofficial policy in Birmingham, at the time of the research, was to summon twice as many men as women. We have since been informed by the Crown Court authorities in Birmingham that this practice, which grew up to counter the likelihood that many females would apply for excusal, has now been discontinued.

[26] The Morris Committee (para. 50) recognized that many women have family responsibilities which make it difficult for them to spare the time for jury service, and saw a 'generous use of the summoning officer's power to excuse' as the solution. It is interesting that a similar practice appears to be followed in many jurisdictions in the United States: see Van Dyke (1977) pp. 121–3.

(particularly the West Indies, India, and Pakistan) and, to a lesser degree, from Ireland. It must immediately be stated that there are numerous difficulties in accurately ascertaining the numbers of the Irish and black populations in the population at large. There is the well-known problem of under-enumeration in the census, to which reference has already been made. There is the unknown influence of the five-year residence qualification which also affects the comparison in some measure. Nor do the census figures offer a breakdown in terms of relevant age-groups. Finally, there is likely to be in some cases a language difficulty, especially with the Asian community, which would again reduce the numbers eligible for jury service. These problems, and there are others, make straightforward comparisons hazardous. This said, however, it is difficult to reconcile the fact that only 28 out of 3,912 jurors in Birmingham (0·7 per cent) were of West Indian or Asian origin when, according to estimates derived from the 1976 survey of households in Birmingham as well as the 1971 census, one would have expected twelve or even fifteen times that number for a city like Birmingham. A similar, though less marked disparity was evident with those of Irish origin. The 1976 survey indicated that almost 10 per cent of the city's population originated either from Northern Ireland or from the Irish Republic and, though there are again severe problems of definition and of enumeration, one would nevertheless have expected more of Irish origin on Birmingham juries than the 139 (3·6 per cent) we actually found. It is hard to explain these differences. Although a summoning officer has power to excuse a person from jury service, the circumstances under which excusals may be granted are circumscribed. This would seem to follow from the Practice Direction issued by the Lord Chief Justice in 1973:[27]

A jury consists of 12 individuals chosen at random from the appropriate panel. A juror should be excused if he is personally concerned in the facts of the particular case, or closely connected with a party to the proceedings or with a prospective witness . . . It is contrary to established practice for jurors to be excused on more general grounds such as race, religion, or political beliefs or occupation.

---

[27] See [1973] 1 All E.R. 240. See, here, Dashwood (1974) at pp. 253–4, and Dickey (1974).

Nor do challenges to jurors affect the question. Only one black juror appeared to have been challenged on the basis of his race—by a West Indian defendant. The reasons for this imbalance on Birmingham juries need to be investigated by the relevant authorities.

This brings us to the important question of the ways that variations in jury composition might produce different verdicts. To put the question another way: how far are the questionable verdicts which were described in Chapters 4 and 5 explicable in terms of the social background of the jurors themselves? There has been an enormous amount of legal writing and speculation on this subject, not to mention a smattering of legal, psychological, and sociological research. There have certainly been in history numerous instances of 'rogue' juries, often deliberately constituted to produce wayward verdicts, but the more important question concerns over-all patterns and consistent trends that might be discernible. With the information on the background of jurors in Birmingham specially collected for us by the Crown Court authorities, we were able to investigate, using real not simulated jurors, the extent to which the verdicts returned were related to such factors as the age, sex, occupation, race, and previous jury experience of the jurors trying the case.

Questions such as whether all-male or all-white juries produce different results from other juries may at first sight seem simple enough to answer. Close investigation, however, shows them to be extremely complex. For not only is the information on social background that we have collected rudimentary,[28] but the particular classifications one adopts of juries as, say, predominantly young or middle-class, may have a critical (but unknown) bearing on the results obtained. Thus, an exclusively middle-class jury may well decide issues differently from a jury composed entirely of manual workers, but 'pure' juries of each type are extremely rare and, for all practical purposes, it is necessary to look for trends based on juries which are *more or less* middle-class or *predominantly* working-class. This requires an analysis of some sophistication: it also necessitates an elaborate

---

[28] We have no information, for instance, on the educational background of jurors nor on their religion or political attitudes, though these factors may have some influence on the verdict returned.

manipulation of data based on many separate breakdowns using several different classifications. Even when this laborious exercise has been conducted, it may be the case that a particular combination of attributes, and no single one, may have an important effect. To take an absurd example, it may be that juries which include three or more older, Irish, non-manual women deliver verdicts consistently more lenient (or more savage) than those of other juries.

Despite these qualifications the interesting point to emerge from our examination of the social background of jurors was that, however one regarded the material, no consistent patterns were apparent. This is a surprising finding not only because it seems to conflict with rules-of-thumb adopted by many experienced lawyers in the courts, but more particularly because it contradicts so much writing and research on the subject. It is, therefore, necessary to look carefully at the results obtained. Before discussing these in detail, it is important to note that the basis of the examination is the number of jury *trials*, not the number of defendants tried. To have used the latter measure would have seriously distorted the picture by artificially inflating the importance of those trials in which there were multiple defendants. Furthermore, since we are concerned in this exercise with those outcomes actually determined by jury, we have excluded the fifty juries empanelled in those cases in which there was an acquittal directed by the judge or in which the defendant changed his plea to guilty in the course of the trial. Bearing these considerations in mind, we shall examine the influence of jury composition on the verdict returned.

Much has been written over the years about the desirability, or otherwise, of having women on juries, though there is a certain ambivalence about which side is likely to be favoured as a result. The majority view seems to be that women will tend to be more sympathetic to the defence than men, with the exception of cases involving sexual offences. The available research evidence, derived almost entirely from simulated jury experiments, is no less ambivalent. Simon (1967), for example, found that women tended to be more sympathetic than men towards the defendant in cases involving house-breaking, though more severe than men in incest cases. Some researchers have noted that, in civil cases, there is likely to be a considerable benefit to the litigant, particularly the low-status litigant, from having females on the jury, whereas others have produced an opposite result.[29] Fortunately, the results of our research in Birmingham were much more clear-cut. However one approached the question, and whatever yardstick was used to measure female representation, no significant variations were found in the verdicts returned. Of the 276 trials examined, 18 involved all-male juries. The acquittal rate of these 18 juries was slightly lower than the average for all juries. On the other hand, six or more women (and in one case ten) sat on 35 juries and it is interesting to note that their acquittal rate was even lower than that of the 18 all-male juries. If one examines the outcome of those cases in which there were at least four women sitting on the jury, the acquittal rate corresponds pretty well exactly to the city average. Nor were any significant variations found in terms of the questionable verdicts returned by juries on which females were well represented. In other words, the possibility that the questionable verdicts discussed in Chapters 4 and 5 of this book may be explicable in terms of the numbers of women sitting on juries can safely be dismissed. The conclusion to be derived from this examination is that, as a rule, the presence of women in any numbers is not likely, *per se*, to change the nature of the verdict returned.

More or less the same result was obtained with respect to age. This is particularly interesting since young jurors have traditionally been assumed to be much more sympathetically inclined towards the defence than are older jurors. This assumption appears to have been buttressed by the common-sense observation that younger jurors are more likely to identify with defendants, most of whom are relatively young.[30] It is also supported by research, and Sealy and Cornish (1973a), to take perhaps the best example, note that:

[29] Snyder (1971) conducted an interesting study concerned with the effect of admitting for the first time women on to juries in civil cases in South Carolina. She found that the 'inferior-status litigant' won the same number of decisions as did the 'superior-status litigant' when confronting male–female juries whereas, when confronting an all-male jury, those of inferior status won a significantly lower proportion of decisions. Paradoxically, she found that financial damages awarded by all-male juries were higher than those awarded by male–female juries. See also Miller (1922); Nagel and Weitzman (1972); Sealy and Cornish (1973a); and Stephan (1975) at pp. 109–15.

[30] See the discussion on this question in the Morris Report (1965) at paras. 69–76, the Note, *Journal of Criminal Law and Criminology* (1975), and in Van Dyke (1977).

the most striking aspect of the various results has been that an association appears in more than one of the different trials only between the youth of the jurors and their verdicts . . . it seems fair to suggest that the inclusion or exclusion of particular social groups [for jury service] will have no generally predictable effect, except in relation to the prescribed minimum age. (pp. 507–8.)

Our research in Birmingham did not confirm this association between young jurors and levels of acquittal. We found that the age structure of juries had no effect whatever on the outcome of cases. We did not find any evidence to suggest that those juries involved in outcomes we have classified as questionable, or in acquittals in general, were younger on average than others. Looking at the question in a different way, we can also say that those juries which contain relatively large numbers of young jurors are not significantly more likely to produce acquittals or questionable verdicts than other juries. The results thus indicate that the age composition of juries in Birmingham was not a significant factor in the verdicts that were returned.

The relationship between the social class of jurors and their verdicts is a more complex one to disentangle, not just because the variable of social class is itself notoriously difficult to define and to measure,[31] but more generally because, in the present context, there are so many ways of measuring the representation of different social classes on individual juries. Such difficulties are inevitably reflected both in the literature on the subject and in the results of the available research. There is a common assumption that jurors of lower socio-economic status will generally be sympathetic towards the defence, though the research evidence, taken as a whole, scarcely supports any firm conclusion on the question.[32] In Birmingham, the main difficulty encountered in reaching a cut-and-dried answer is simply that, since so few juries can be accurately classified as either *largely* middle-class or *largely* working-class, the variations in the outcome of different types of jury are bound to be difficult to detect. Having said this, and having examined the phenomenon of social class from as many angles as the informa-

[31] There is a large literature on these problems. Useful discussions are given in Goldthorpe and Hope (1974) and Reid (1977).

[32] There is a good deal of inconsistency in the research evidence: see, Broeder (1965b); Simon (1967); Note, *Stanford Law Review* (1969); Hermann (1970); Adler (1973); Sealy and Cornish (1973a); Stephan (1975); and Van Dyke (1977).

tion at hand would allow, we concluded that it was not a significant influence on jury verdicts. Table 12 presents the results for all verdicts, for all acquittals, and for all questionable outcomes using one of the many possible measures.

TABLE 12

Verdicts of juries related to the proportion of working-class members of the jury

	All jury trials (%)		Acquittals (%)		All questionable outcomes (%)	
Less than 25% of jury working-class	2	0·7	1	1·2	1	2·9
25% less than 50% working-class	53	19·2	16	19·3	10	28·6
50% less than 75% working-class	142	51·5	43	51·8	16	45·7
75% or more of jury working-class	79	28·6	23	27·7	8	22·8
	276	100·0	83	100·0	35	100·0

Much discussion has been taken up in recent years with the racial composition of juries, and in some cases black defendants have claimed the right to be tried by an all-black jury.[33] In our study, an examination of the relationship between the racial composition of juries and their verdicts is limited by the fact that so few individuals of non-British origin sat on juries, let alone on the same juries, in the period of the research. Of the 276 juries in question, only eleven included three or more members of non-British origin, and on only one jury did two jurors of New Commonwealth origin sit together. The juries which included individuals of non-British origin had a lower rate of acquittal, and returned proportionately fewer verdicts within our category of questionable outcomes, than the all-British juries but in neither case was the difference statistically significant. No firm conclusions can be drawn from this comparison as to the effect of race in relation to the verdicts returned, given the small numbers involved.

A final hypothesis that can be examined in relation to the information supplied by the Crown Court on the background of jurors concerns the frequently encountered assumption that

[33] See, for example, *Broderick* [1970] Crim. L.R. 155. The question is discussed by Dashwood (1972).

jurors trying their first case are much more likely to acquit—and to acquit perversely—than more experienced jurors. This has become widely known in England as the 'first-day syndrome' and it is by no means unknown in the United States.[34] The position is graphically stated by a juror in the following passage:[35]

. . . acquittals were more frequent while jurors were green. If you are an accused you will do well to have your case first on the list. At that stage plenty of jurymen will believe that there is reasonable doubt if no one has actually seen you with your hand in the till. If, after long argument and with several of them still doubtful, they find you guilty and then discover that you have seventeen previous convictions for similar offences, scales tend to drop from their eyes; they become old soldiers overnight and the next accused is viewed much more circumspectly.

In Birmingham, only one juror in three had had previous experience in an earlier trial during his current term of service, and over 40 per cent of juries consisted entirely of individuals without such experience. Indeed, only 20 per cent of juries included even one member who had sat on two or more previous cases. It emerged from our examination of jurors' backgrounds that the least experienced juries produced a lower proportion of questionable outcomes than other juries, though the differences did not reach a level of statistical significance. We can conclude that, though juries in Birmingham were composed largely of inexperienced individuals, this cannot be taken to explain the relatively large proportion of jury outcomes classified as questionable which have been discussed in Chapters 4 and 5 of this book.

Having examined the relationships between the characteristics of juries and the verdicts they return, we can confidently state that no single social factor (nor, as far as we could detect, any group of factors operating in combination) produced any significant variation in the verdicts returned across the board. This negative conclusion is, to a degree, a surprising one since common sense and a voluminous literature would have suggested the opposite. The contradiction is, however, relatively

[34] Some empirical support for the proposition is given in Broeder (1965c).
[35] In Barber and Gordon (1976) at pp. 97–8 (see also ibid. pp. 110, 167–8).

easily explained. The truth of the matter is that most juries in Birmingham were extremely mixed, and it is to be expected that the amalgam of personal and social attributes that make up a jury will produce verdicts which reflect that unique social mix rather than the broad social characteristics of the individuals concerned.[36] It is relatively easy in a laboratory to produce juries of young people or of women or of white-collar workers but these are only very exceptionally reproduced in the court room. Even the right to challenge individual jurors, which might on occasion make for a somewhat artificially constituted panel, only very rarely had this effect. In the final analysis, it seems that individual attitudes and prejudices, as they are manifested in relation to the particular questions at issue, are more crucial in understanding the final verdict returned than general social characteristics.

[36] A similar conclusion was reached by Simon (1967) in her exhaustive study of the way that juries dealt with the defence of insanity in a series of mock jury trials. She writes: 'In any situation what a person thinks or does is a function of who he is, the exigencies of the situation, how strongly he feels about the problem, and a host of other factors' (p. 118.)

7

PROFESSIONAL CRIMINALS AND
THE TRIAL SYSTEM

In recent years in England, the debate surrounding trial by jury has not been confined to the question whether too many guilty people are acquitted: much of the discussion has turned on the sorts of defendant who manage to obtain acquittals. More specifically, it has sometimes been argued that it is the professional criminal who is best able to manipulate the trial system to his own advantage and who is thereby most likely to be able to gain an acquittal before a jury. The Criminal Law Revision Committee in their 11th report on *Evidence* (1972), to take the most widely debated example, accepted the proposition that professional criminals posed a particular threat to the criminal justice system:

There is now a large and increasing class of sophisticated professional criminals who are not only highly skilful in organising their crimes and in the steps they take to avoid detection but are well aware of their legal rights and use every possible means to avoid conviction if caught. (para. 21.)

The Committee's proposals, to dismantle the accused's right of silence and to allow in limited circumstances details of previous convictions to be admitted in evidence, were undermined mainly because of the lack of any empirical support for their contentions. Many of their critics felt the proposals to be too heavily influenced by the Committee's unfounded hunches and assumptions about the abilities of professional criminals to thwart the trial system.[1] At more or less the same time, Sir Robert Mark, the then Metropolitan Commissioner of Police, launched a more direct assault on the jury system, drawing particular attention to the problems it posed with regard to the proper conviction of professional criminals. According to Mark, only a small proportion of those acquitted by juries were

[1] See, for instance, the critical reports of the General Council of the Bar (1973); the National Council for Civil Liberties (1973); and the Release Lawyers' Group (1973).

likely to be innocent in the true sense of the word and, under the existing system, it was the professional criminal who was 'the very man most likely to escape society's protective net'.[2] It is only recently that research evidence has been brought to bear upon these issues.

The first investigation, conducted by Zander (1974a), was conceived as a direct response to the statements of the Criminal Law Revision Committee and of Sir Robert Mark. Zander's study, to which reference was made in Chapter 1 of this book, concerned cases heard in the Central Criminal Court and the Inner London Crown Court. He was interested to test the proposition that professional criminals represent a significant proportion of all acquitted defendants and that they are more likely than others to avoid conviction. The answer to this question clearly depended upon the definition of 'professional criminals'. The term has no fixed meaning and Zander discussed a number of possible definitions of it. In his analysis, he decided to use two. Under his first definition, a professional was simply someone with a substantial criminal record, whilst under the second definition, professionalism was confined to 'crime of the more serious variety, involving gangs, organisation, firearms or other dangerous weapons and the whole paraphernalia of stolen getaway cars, gloves, ammonia, stocking masks, etc.'.[3] Applying his first measure, Zander found that a significantly higher proportion of those convicted had previous convictions than of those acquitted, and that the longer the criminal record, the lower the acquittal rate. His second measure showed that the proportion of serious cases in the sample of acquittals was relatively low (19 per cent). In summary, Zander concluded that:

[T]he evidence shows that the defendant with a prior record has a statistically lower rather than a higher chance of an acquittal than someone with no conviction. It would not seem therefore that the system is by its nature tipped in favour of the professional criminal. (p. 60.)

Zander's findings were highly contentious and his conclusions were immediately subjected to criticism. The details of

[2] Mark (1972) p. 13.
[3] Zander (1974a) p. 35.

the dispute need not concern us here but the central issue is important.[4] Whilst Zander's findings constitute strong evidence that those with long criminal records are not more likely than other defendants to avoid conviction, it is difficult to accept that this tells us anything about professional criminals. As Mack (1976) put it: '. . . a substantial record is neither a necessary nor a sufficient condition of acceptance or labelling as a professional criminal' (p. 246). It is undoubtedly true that many professionals have a substantial criminal record, but several studies show that a long criminal record is at least as likely to be indicative of personal inadequacy and fecklessness as of professionalism.[5] Conversely, it is likely that some professional criminals are able to avoid conviction for long periods of time and would, on that account, be exluded from Zander's definition. In short, the substantial record definition of professional criminals must be treated as largely irrelevant to the debate. The second definition adopted by Zander, based upon the characteristic features of professional criminal activity, raises fewer difficulties of this nature. Few would disagree that criminals who use stolen getaway cars, ammonia, masks, and the like are serious enough, but the application of criteria of this kind to the circumstances of particular crimes is notoriously difficult to achieve,[6] and we are ourselves by no means convinced that Zander managed to apply his definition in a uniform way.[7] Zander's study, though providing some important material on the separate issue of jury perversity, cannot be said to have shed much light on the narrower question of the relative immunity of professional criminals from conviction by jury.

The study by Mack (1976) was somewhat more successful in this regard. Mack sought to identify professional criminals by

[4] The issues are dealt with in Baldwin and McConville (1974) and Zander (1974b).

[5] See, for example, Hammond and Chayen (1963), and West (1963) who writes: 'Those professional crooks whose operations constitute the most serious menace to valuable property are most likely to be found outside of prison' (p. 104). For other views of what is meant by 'professional crime', see Cressey (1972); McIntosh (1975); and Mack (1975).

[6] The problems of defining what is meant by serious crime are well known to criminologists: see, for instance, Wolfgang and Sellin (1964), and McClintock and Avison (1968) at pp. 56–9.

[7] For further details of our doubts on this point, see Baldwin and McConville (1974) at pp. 440–1.

obtaining from the police details of those regarded as requiring 'special attention'—active full-time criminals who were likely to involve themselves in criminal enterprises. After cross-checking with 'in-group' criminals, Mack was confident that the group so identified by the police included the major criminals in the area of study. Mack described the typical professional criminal with whom he was concerned as:

... the full-time, major, skilled operator; the man who has made crime his occupation or profession and gets the greater part of his income and his main interest in life from his work, who usually undertakes criminal operations of some size, and who has more than average skill in the planning and execution of these operations.(p. 247.)

Apart from this group (which he terms the Main Group), Mack identified two other groups, neither of which was viewed as consisting of professional crooks. These groups were the Lesser Group (full-time operators with less expertise and involved for the most part in small-scale activities) and the Small Fry (non-professionals but sometimes full-time petty operators). His principal method of comparing the fortunes of different groups was to calculate the number of charges made which did not result in a conviction as a proportion of the total of the charges. His results showed that, on average, the Small Fry were convicted on 85 per cent of charges brought against them, the Lesser Group on 80 per cent, and the Main Group of professional criminals on 75 per cent. If one accepts the validity of the comparisons made,[8] it is difficult, on the evidence he adduces, to share Mack's concern about the ability of professional crooks to beat the system. If professional criminals are distinguished by their expertise and skill, one would expect them to be much more successful in manipulating the system than are other groups, but on Mack's figures their comparative success in this regard is slight. His evidence that professional criminals avoid the impact of the criminal law somewhat more often than do other criminals is of importance, but his findings scarcely justify his conclusion that the rules of evidence should accordingly be widened to allow evidence of the defendant's social history, life-style, and the like to be admitted at trial.

[8] Mack's approach in this regard has been challenged by Sanders (1977).

Our approach to the question of professional crime differs from that of Zander and of Mack. As we indicated in Chapter 2, we derived our information on professional crime from the police by means of structured questionnaires. For each defendant who fell within our samples (2,406 in Birmingham and 2,292 in London), we asked the police for details of any previous criminal convictions, of any prior acquittals, and of the total period of time to which he had been previously sentenced to terms of imprisonment. In addition, the police provided details of the suspected involvement of each defendant in serious criminal activity that had not been the subject of criminal prosecution, and gave their opinions on a four-point scale of the level of skill and expertise demonstrated by each defendant in his criminal activities; his suspected involvement in organized crime (i.e. crime involving gangs, planning, use of weapons and equipment, etc.); the extent to which a defendant was believed to make a living out of crime; and the extent to which he was prepared to use every possible means, legal and illegal, to avoid conviction. Space was also provided on the questionnaire for other comments any officer might wish to add about a particular defendant. This often produced very forthright views and the following four examples give some idea of the sort of problems that the police see presented by those at the top end of the professionalism scale:

Case 757 (Birmingham) This man systematically uses violence. He is well known for explosives and for being the 'safeman' for particular teams of thieves.

Case 911 (Birmingham) This man can only be described as a scourge to society. He is a dual personality, a criminal Jekyll and Hyde. When he is incarcerated he becomes a model prisoner, is immediately respectful of rules, regulations and authority, but like the cunning fox always waiting for the day of his release so that he can resort to his former life of deceit, crime and a total disregard for a civilized community. This man never has, and never will, lead a normal industrious life.

Case 776 (London) This defendant is an individualist in his criminal activities and as such is not involved in organized crime. His criminal record consists of nothing but sophisticated frauds which necessitate detailed planning and the assistance of other criminals.

It is clear that he has access to, and avails himself of, such assistance.

Case 830 (London) He is a major East London criminal who has the ability to corrupt others and is prepared to use any methods to realize his own ends.

Although the concept of professional crime is a very imprecise one, we believe that the indices we have used (particularly when they are aggregated into an over-all measure), combined with the qualitative information given by the police, provide measurements which, though obviously imperfect, are about as close as one can get to a picture of what is usually meant by professional criminal activity.

It is perhaps useful at this point to present a general view of the extent to which defendants in Birmingham and London were seen by the police as professionals. As noted earlier, the individual indices of professional criminal involvement that we used (living on the proceeds of crime, the degree of skill in criminal enterprises, etc.) were measured on a four-point scale and subsequently amalgamated into an over-all professionalism score. Table 13 presents a comparison of the amalgamated professionalism scores of defendants involved in questionable acquittals, compared to the scores for other defendants who pleaded not guilty and others who pleaded guilty for both Birmingham and London.[9]

Table 13 demonstrates that, although those who score highly on the aggregated measure appear on occasions to be acquitted in questionable circumstances in both Birmingham and London, there is no tendency for them to be questionably acquitted more often than other defendants. It is clear that, in Birmingham at least, a substantial majority of professional criminals actually plead guilty at trial. We can say, then, that only a miniscule proportion of all cases end in the questionable acquittal of any defendant who, on the measures used here, could be regarded as a professional criminal. Indeed, of those scoring highly on the professionalism scale in each city, no more than one in eighty was said to have been questionably acquitted. At the same time, none of the defendants involved in

[9] In the table for London, 12 cases are excluded because no plea was entered by the defendants in question.

questionable convictions was seen by the police as a professional criminal.

The broad picture appears clear-cut and it puts the debate about professional criminals into perspective. But it is necessary to examine the question in greater detail, for Table 13

TABLE 13

Police assessments of levels of involvement in professional criminal activity

(a) Birmingham defendants

Professionalism score	Questionable acquittals		Other contested cases		Guilty pleas		All defendants	
		(%)		(%)		(%)		(%)
Low	27	65·8	200	44·3	937	50·4	1,164	49·5
Medium	8	19·5	156	34·6	614	33·0	778	33·1
High	2	4·9	69	15·3	243	13·1	314	13·3
Very high	4	9·8	26	5·8	66	3·5	96	4·1
Not known	0	–	8	–	46	–	54	–
	41	100·0	459	100·0	1,906	100·0	2,406	100·0

(b) London defendants

Professionalism score	Questionable acquittals		Other contested cases		Guilty pleas		All defendants	
		(%)		(%)		(%)		(%)
Low	22	59·5	614	51·7	465	46·0	1,101	49·2
Medium	10	27·0	331	27·9	329	32·5	670	30·0
High	4	10·8	167	14·1	162	16·0	333	14·9
Very high	1	2·7	75	6·3	55	5·5	131	5·9
Not known	2	–	37	–	6	–	45	–
	39	100·0	1,224	100·0	1,017	100·0	2,280	100·0

gives an inadequate representation of the findings and the bald figures mask some important patterns. Thus, for example, the concern voiced by the police and others in the debate has been mainly about the hard core of organized criminals who, by their readiness to resort to violence, represent a special danger to society. It is clear, however, that the group of defendants scoring very highly on the professionalism scale includes many individuals who do not represent such a danger. What the group consists of are rather those seen by the police as skilful and relatively successful crooks, only a minority of whom use violence as their stock-in-trade. But there are within this group a small number of individuals who would appear to pose a more serious threat to the public, and it is particularly important to examine what happens to this group when they appear in court.

Although Table 13 appears to show that the concern that has frequently been expressed about the ability of professional crooks to manipulate the criminal justice system to their own advantage is in large part misplaced, a number of somewhat surprising findings have emerged in the course of our inquiry which, taken in isolation, might help to explain how these fears were generated in the first place. This information is derived from a comparison of the nature of the charges brought in the current case and the degree of professionalism of the defendant; from an analysis of the previous criminal history of professional crooks and their previous involvement with the courts; and from the allegations of malpractice, and even corruption, against lawyers associated with such defendants made by police officers in the interviews we conducted.

If it were the case that professional criminals were by definition particularly skilful operators, one would expect them to be able to manipulate the system at every stage of the criminal process. In other words, if they were better able to secure acquittals than other groups of defendants, one would also anticipate that they would be more adept at avoiding detection and apprehension and also that they would be more successful in minimizing the seriousness of the charges brought where they have been arrested. There is no doubt that many of those identified by the police both in Birmingham and in London made apprehension extremely difficult for the police. Officers in both cities frequently commented on their inability to gather sufficient evidence to charge a defendant, and these comments were almost entirely restricted to the professional crooks. The following comments are typical of the difficulties the police apparently encounter in such cases:

Case 336 (London) He will make allegations of a most serious nature against the police (i.e. corruption) and use the Press for this purpose to cloud the issue in a trial and gain sympathy from the judge and jury. He then fails to substantiate allegations when they have served their purpose. He always uses the services of much lesser criminals who invariably get arrested whilst he goes free.

Case 848 (London) He is a professional shoplifter. He uses hired cars and travels throughout the Home Counties stealing clothing and then obtaining refunds. He was acquitted because others involved accepted full responsibility, pleaded guilty and then gave evidence on his behalf.

Case 2192 (London) He is involved in the background of large-scale robberies and frauds, without seemingly taking an active part in the offences themselves. He is suspected of the redistribution of stolen money but there is insufficient evidence to charge.

Case 398 (Birmingham) He is suspected for numerous different offences involving large-scale thefts and burglaries and he has been arrested several times. He is, however, difficult to deal with and on recent occasions it has been impossible to charge him with these offences. He admits nothing.

Case 1850 (Birmingham) My inquiries show that there has been insufficient evidence to date to proceed against him. It is known that he associates with criminals, organizing burglaries and receiving stolen property. He is also involved with juveniles in crime. His associates fear him.

It is clear from these comments that the police often experience particular problems in apprehending those whom they believe to be deeply involved in the business of crime. Equally, if the police suspicions of this involvement are correct, it is apparent that, when they do apprehend the defendant in question, the charges that they are able to bring are sometimes comparatively trivial. In both cities, for example, a number of defendants who were suspected of being involved in large-scale burglaries or thefts faced, in the current case, charges relating to relatively minor theft or handling. It does not follow, therefore, that the questionable acquittal of such defendants represents less of a threat to the public simply because the offence in question was of a non-serious nature. In assessing the risks to the community at large, it is proper in such cases to go beyond the circumstances of the particular offence. There is some evidence from the police that certain professional crooks are able to avoid apprehension, or at least to minimize the seriousness of the charges they face, for long periods. To that extent, one can argue that the concerns referred to earlier should not be dismissed out of hand.

The second source of information relevant to the disquiet over professional crooks is derived from an analysis of their prior criminal histories and their previous encounters with the courts and the penal system, disregarding the outcome of the current case. In both London and Birmingham, professional criminals were found to have had a greater number of prior convictions than was the case with other groups of defendants;[10] they had been sentenced to prison more frequently; and they had secured a higher proportion of acquittals. There were, however, some variations between the two cities in that professional criminals in London on the whole fared better than those in Birmingham. In London, almost 20 per cent of the professional group had no prior convictions whatever, whereas this applied to only about 8 per cent in Birmingham.[11] More than half the professionals had served less than a year in prison altogether, and 40 per cent had never been to prison at all. It is clear, then, that whatever the fortunes of professional criminals in securing acquittals in court, perversely or otherwise, they seemed in many cases able to minimize the impact of the criminal process and, with considerable success, to avoid the imposition of harsh penalties.

On the question of previous acquittals, some interesting results emerged. Senior police officers have argued, specifically in relation to the professionals, that many are able to gain a disproportionate number of acquittals before they are eventually convicted. The point has been forcibly made on a number of occasions by Sir Robert Mark, as in the following passage:[12]

To pray in aid the eventual conviction of [serious criminals] surely illustrates the complacency which the present system encourages. It

[10] It is not perhaps surprising to find that professionals as a group are more likely to have been previously convicted of criminal offences and to have served sentences of imprisonment than have other defendants, for this is largely due to the fact that they are more likely to have been involved in larger criminal enterprises and thus to have exposed themselves to greater risks of imprisonment than others. See also Mack (1976) pp. 252–3, who found that the full-time, major criminals had a proportionately smaller prison-free ratio than other groups.

[11] 52 per cent of professionals in London, and 68 per cent in Birmingham, had at least five convictions, and there were numerous individuals in both cities who were placed low on the professionalism scale yet had amassed very many previous convictions.

[12] 'Reply to Lord Wigoder', *The Observer*, 6 April 1975. See also Mark (1973) at p. 16.

would be much more to the point to mention, in respect of notorious wrongdoers of that kind, the often remarkable number of acquittals on their road to eventual conviction . . . [A]ny experienced Old Bailey counsel is able to call to mind notorious criminals whose eventual downfall was prefaced by a number of acquittals, which no doubt encouraged them in their criminal activities.

Taking all defendants in London on which information on previous acquittals was available, 342 defendants (15 per cent) had been acquitted on one or more occasions in the past. An analysis of the patterns of acquittal obtained by these defendants lends some support to Mark's view. Professional criminals (n = 131), who comprised some 6 per cent of all defendants, secured over 16 per cent of the prior acquittals. Looking at the question in another way, 14 per cent of the non-professionals had been previously acquitted whereas no fewer than 42 per cent (n = 56) of the professionals, had prior acquittals. The same pattern held for Birmingham, although no more than 80 of all defendants had on earlier occasions been acquitted. In Birmingham, professional criminals (n = 96) comprised about 4 per cent of all defendants yet they secured about 18 per cent of all prior acquittals. No more than 3 per cent of the non-professionals had been previously acquitted. It is likely, therefore, that, by reason of their expertise in carrying out criminal ventures and the relative difficulty the police have in gathering evidence against them, professional criminals are, more easily than other groups, able to secure acquittals. But the support this gives to Mark's thesis is limited because professionals are also more likely to have a criminal record, and this suggests that their disproportionate share of prior acquittals is explained in part by the fact that they have been more frequently exposed to the risk of conviction in the past. In any event, only a small proportion of defendants in both cities had been acquitted on previous occasions with any frequency. In fact, taking together all defendants in Birmingham and London, less than one defendant in ten had secured an acquittal on a previous occasion and only a small minority of these had done so more than once.

The third source of information relates to allegations of corruption made to us by the police in relation to the practices of certain lawyers. In the 1973 Dimbleby Lecture, Sir Robert

Mark said that acquittals arising from humanitarian considerations were much rarer than one might suppose and that more frequent were cases where the criminal and his lawyer exploited the defects and uncertainties in the rules of evidence and procedure. He argued that there was a small minority of criminal lawyers who concocted sophisticated defences for their clients, produced false alibis, and introduced into the trial extraneous issues damaging to police credibility. In a highly controversial passage, he concluded:

Let there be no doubt that a minority of criminal lawyers do very well from the proceeds of crime . . . Experienced and respected metropolitan detectives can identify lawyers in criminal practice who are more harmful to society than the clients they represent. (p. 12.)

These startling allegations produced a vigorous reaction from members of the legal profession[13] and the controversy was fuelled when, in 1977, it emerged that the Metropolitan Police actually had a 'blacklist' of lawyers who were suspected of putting up false defences on behalf of certain criminals.[14] The Law Society had previously pointed out that the existence of a suspicion that a small minority of lawyers offend against the rules was insufficient reason for subjecting the whole profession to 'a general smear',[15] and they now made it clear that, if the police were unable to make their allegations stick, there was little chance that the Law Society could do so either.[16]

This subject is one on which our own inquiry sheds a little light. Though we have not been able to obtain a copy of the

[13] See, for instance, *Law Society Gazette*, 26 March 1975, where Sir David Napley (acting as spokesman for the Law Society) is reported to have said: 'The real cause for concern is not merely that Sir Robert had made another attack on the lawyers who, otherwise, throughout the country had good personal relations with the police whom they admired, and which his repeated outbursts were liable to destroy; the real concern was that someone in his position should by general smears undermine the confidence of the public by attacking those who practise the law, at a time when the public interest requires all responsible persons to support the rule of law against those who seek to destroy it.'

[14] See the *Sunday Times*, 13 March 1977; *The Times*, 14 March 1977.

[15] See *Guardian Gazette*, 26 March 1975, and also Morton (1977) who writes: 'If there is anything in the complaint then it can be dealt with, if it is unsubstantiated then the Law Society should crack down on behalf of the profession on what is, after all, a trial by smear without any evidence being produced . . .' (p. 280).

[16] *The Times*, 14 March 1977. We have been informed by the Metropolitan Police Force, however, that in recent years a number of successful prosecutions against London solicitors have been launched.

'blacklist' of lawyers, we have collected some information relevant to the sensitive question of professional malpractice of the kind described by Mark. This information emerged spontaneously in the course of interviewing police officers and from asking them to provide details of the criminal background of all defendants in the sample. It is abundantly clear from these sources that, if there is a problem of corrupt lawyers, it is of very small proportions and confined to London. In the whole of the Birmingham sample, there was not a single serious allegation of any practice which could possibly be described as corrupt. Not surprisingly, solicitors and barristers were frequently criticized by police officers but only in so far as they were, in their view, bad at their job. Some solicitors were picked out for their enthusiasm in defending their clients' interests and the police sometimes saw them as nuisances, creating unwarranted difficulties to proving a case. Only two individual solicitors in Birmingham were ever alleged by police officers to have acted in a manner that might be seen as legally or morally dubious, but even in these isolated instances, there was no serious hint of corrupt practice. As far as Birmingham solicitors are concerned, then, allegations by the police of serious malpractice were not encountered in relation to any of the cases examined. In the overwhelming majority of cases, the same could be said of London. In a small number of cases, however, individual officers spontaneously proffered, in the interviews we conducted, allegations of a serious nature against certain lawyers. In all, twelve firms of solicitors in London were said to be corrupt in one way or another. Before giving examples of the sort of comments that were made to us, we should emphasize that these remain, in the absence of supporting evidence, no more than allegations. Nevertheless, the facts that they emanate from responsible and experienced police officers, that they relate to specific cases, and that they form a distinctive pattern force us to take them seriously. At the very least, they support the sincerely felt concerns of senior police officers of the Metropolitan Force and do not by any stretch of the imagination represent 'generalized smears' against the legal profession as a whole. The comments, in our view, cannot be dismissed out of hand. The following are representative of the allegations made by London officers, when interviewed about specific cases:

Case 44 [The defendant was convicted of theft and deception]
  On the morning of the trial, the defence solicitors presented me
  with a notice of alibi, three months late. The solicitors, who are
  bent, said in court that the defendant had presented him with the
  alibi before the seven day period had elapsed and that he had
  mistakenly forgotten to submit it. This was a lie—they are a
  notorious firm of bent solicitors.

Case 205 [The defendant was acquitted of conspiracy to defraud]
  This defendant is a highly successful professional criminal, involved
  with American organized criminals. He is advised by [a solicitor]
  and this combination is dangerous, motivated by money and
  completely anti-social. If you are dealing with a wealthy, professional criminal like this man, all the lawyers are interested in him.
  This case was a carve-up from beginning to end. At the start, both
  prosecution and defence counsel were from the same chambers.
  Prosecuting counsel dropped the case half-way through and
  handed it over to a colleague who failed to grasp the complexities of
  the case: this was a deliberate ploy, all part of the carve-up. Where
  large sums of money are paid to counsel by professional criminals
  on condition that they are acquitted, some barristers will stop at
  nothing.

Case 229 [The defendant was convicted of theft]
  The defendant is a well-known, obstructive and professional vil-
  lain. He is a unique criminal, gaining a series of acquittals over the
  years. He always employs unique and novel defences and has the
  assistance of dubious lawyers who are as much a bunch of crooks as
  those he hangs around with.

Case 344 [A case in which the defendant was acquitted of theft on the
  direction of the judge]
  The prosecuting and defence lawyers decided to end the case
  before it even came to court. I overheard conversations and I know
  that there was bribery of the prosecuting counsel. The lawyers
  were on the take.

Many people will not be surprised that, if lawyers were to be
accused of engaging in corrupt practices, the charges should
emanate primarily from London. Some will no doubt believe
that Metropolitan police officers would react in this way
because they have been sensitized to the problem by their then
Commissioner, Sir Robert Mark. Others would perhaps argue
that it is quite reasonable to expect that some criminals will

attempt to purchase immunity from the criminal process, particularly in the case of large-scale operators in London.[17] There
may be some truth in both these views but certain things are
quite clear. In the overwhelming majority of all cases, police
officers made no such allegations and, when they did, they
appeared honestly to believe that they had good grounds for
doing so. In these few cases, they may have been mistaken but
the allegations were not, in our view, ever put forward for
mischievous reasons. Moreover, the allegations made were not
related to the outcome of the case, for in five of the twelve cases
the defendant concerned was convicted. In that sense, at least,
it might be said that the allegations were not recriminatory.[18]
The most telling finding, however, was that, in no fewer than
eleven of these twelve instances, the defendant in question was,
in the opinion of the police, a professional criminal. This cannot
be explained away on the basis that such allegations were made
simply because the defendant was seen as such by the police, for
no allegations whatever were made in relation to the overwhelming majority (92 per cent) of professional criminals. If
these allegations have any substance, some comfort can be
drawn from the fact that the problem is certainly extremely
limited in scope, and that the employment of 'shady' lawyers
does not by any means guarantee for anyone a favourable
outcome at trial.[19]

It is easy to see from the foregoing why it is that certain
pieces of evidence, considered in isolation, might readily generate amongst police officers a genuine concern over the problems
created by professional criminals and, specifically, their success in manipulating the trial system to their own ends. Their
occasional success in avoiding apprehension altogether and in
minimizing the seriousness of the charges brought when
arrested, their ability to secure a disproportionate share of
acquittals over a period of time, and their alleged use of dubious

[17] See, for example, Cressey (1972) at pp. 3–4, and Mack (1976) at pp. 265–7.
[18] Compare Morton (1977): 'There is many a policeman who blames an acquittal
on defence trickiness because either he has not prepared his case properly or has failed
to understand the rules of evidence. Sometimes, however rarely, the defendant is
genuinely innocent' (p. 280).
[19] Cf. Chambliss and Seidman (1971) Chapter 23, where it is argued that professional crooks are able to secure immunity from punishment, especially by means of
bribery.

lawyers to secure acquittal, are all matters which have, quite understandably, exercised the minds of police officers. The results of the present inquiry do, however, suggest that senior police officers have tended to exaggerate the *extent* of what is, no doubt, an extremely serious problem. Once the fortunes of professional criminals across the board are examined, a different picture emerges.

It is clear from Table 13 that the proportion of defendants seen by the police as serious calculating criminals in each city is no more than 6 per cent of all defendants, and that a majority of these plead guilty at trial. In Birmingham, there was a significant tendency for professionals to contest their cases more frequently than other defendants (31 per cent as against 20 per cent), but in London the proportions (58 per cent as against 55 per cent) were not statistically significant. Even though there is some tendency for professional criminals to contest cases more frequently than other defendants, it is nevertheless apparent that, when they plead not guilty, a large majority are convicted. Indeed, in Birmingham, professional criminals as a group were convicted more frequently than any other group of defendants. Of those who contested their cases (n = 30), no fewer than 80 per cent were convicted. In London, professionals were slightly more successful, but even so, of those who contested their cases (n = 76), 63 per cent were convicted. Looking at the over-all success of professional criminals in both cities, therefore, almost 94 per cent in Birmingham and over 78 per cent in London were at the end of the day convicted either on their own plea or else after trial. It is important, in this context, to mention the fate of that small number of individuals within the professional group who appear to pose a particular danger to the public. This group consists of individuals who reached the highest levels on each measure of professionalism used. Altogether there were, in London and Birmingham, 40 such individuals. It is noteworthy, however, that this group fared no better at trial than other professional criminals. Indeed, 24 pleaded guilty and a further eight were convicted after trial. The picture that emerges is thus hardly one of professional criminals exploiting the system: rather the evidence suggests that they are for the most part unable to extract much advantage from it.

The pattern is even clearer when one examines more closely the convictions of the professional criminals. There has been some debate in England over the years about whether there is a relationship between the perceived difficulties in convicting professional criminals and the relative frequency of majority jury verdicts. When Lord Wigoder argued that professional criminals are almost invariably convicted in the criminal courts and convicted by unanimous verdicts,[20] Sir Robert Mark replied that the proportion of majority verdicts nevertheless included a substantial number of very serious cases.[21] We were able to examine this question in relation to the information collected in both London and Birmingham. On the evidence of our research, it is apparent that those who were viewed as professional crooks were in most cases convicted or acquitted by unanimous jury verdicts. In Birmingham, it is interesting to note that there were only fifteen majority verdicts in the whole sample, none of which involved a professional criminal. In London there were 66 majority verdicts in all, only five of which related to professional criminals.

It is important to restate the most striking finding to emerge from our analysis of the fortunes of professional criminals before juries: that it is comparatively rare for them to be acquitted and, even when they are, their acquittal is only exceptionally said to be questionable. Table 13 (page 112) shows that there were only four such cases in Birmingham and one in London.[22] It may be the case, as was pointed out earlier, that some professional criminals, though rightly acquitted on the evidence, are not innocent of the crime alleged, but in such instances the explanation would appear to be that they are better able than others to frustrate the efforts of the police to gather sufficient evidence to gain a conviction.[23]

[20] The *Observer*, 30 March 1975.

[21] The *Observer*, 6 April 1975.

[22] This conclusion tallies with the view of the General Council of the Bar (1973) on this question. They write: 'Our combined experience convinces us that if [sophisticated professional] criminals are escaping justice, it is not in the main because of their ability to misuse the rules of evidence. If the evidence is clear and reliable, juries are very ready to convict where organised and/or violent crime is alleged. . . .' (para. 63.)

[23] The general question of whether professional criminals are able to manipulate the rules of evidence to their own advantage to thwart police inquiries is discussed in detail, within the context of the controversial proposals of the Criminal Law Revision Committee (1972), in Baldwin and McConville (1979).

It has often been argued that many professional criminals choose not to fight cases in court because they are able, as it were, to cut their losses by agreeing to plead guilty in return for offers of a more lenient sentence. There is little doubt that the American criminal justice system is heavily dependent on this kind of 'plea bargaining'.[24] In England, the extent of plea bargaining is more limited though the inducements held out to defendants who plead guilty are nevertheless considerable.[25] It might be supposed, then, that professional criminals would be particularly well placed to derive the maximum benefits by way of plea bargaining. Some writers, such as Newman (1956) and Chambliss (1969), have put forward the hypothesis that plea bargaining procedures benefit the professional crook at the expense of his less sophisticated counterpart. Similarly, it might be anticipated that the greater ability of the professional to minimize the seriousness of the charges which could be brought against him would bring comparable benefits. So far as plea negotiation is concerned, the evidence of our recent study (Baldwin and McConville 1977a) showed that very few professional criminals were able to extract greater benefits than other defendants. The present study tends to confirm this general conclusion. Where professional criminals are convicted, after a plea of guilty or following trial, they are subject to more severe sanctions than is the case with any other group. In London, 32 per cent of all defendants received custodial sentences whereas, for professionals, the equivalent figure was 52 per cent. Similarly, in Birmingham, 51 per cent of all defendants were sentenced to immediate terms of imprisonment, whereas the proportion for professionals was 78 per cent.

That the police should regard the judicial machinery as inadequate to cope with the problems posed by the ruthless and calculating criminal, particularly when he appears before a jury and is aided by lawyers seen as fundamentally untrustworthy, is understandable enough. It is not surprising if the police focus upon the fact that professional criminals do, without doubt, secure spectacular and perverse acquittals from time to time. However understandable these concerns may be, it must

[24] There is a huge literature on this subject. Useful summaries are given in Newman (1966); Whitman (1967); Cooper (1972); and Heberling (1973).
[25] On this, see Baldwin and McConville (1977a and 1978b).

be borne in mind that the present inquiry found such acquittals to be exceptionally infrequent. Although small numbers of professional criminals *are* acquitted in highly questionable circumstances, it nevertheless remains the case that a large proportion plead guilty at trial and, of those who contest their cases, the great majority are convicted, usually by unanimous verdicts. Moreover, professional criminals are more likely than other groups to be given custodial sentences on conviction. As far as the evidence from our own inquiry is concerned, we would conclude that any proposal to change the rules of evidence solely on the basis of the alleged threat posed by professional criminals to the judicial system is misconceived.

8

CONCLUSIONS

OUR aim throughout this book has been to provide a factual framework, based upon the empirical analysis of a considerable number of contested trials, which might serve to inform discussions about the future of trial by jury. The framework we have sought to provide is limited both in the sense that it is not strictly relevant to some of the issues in the jury debate (such as the jury's political function), and in the sense that the research methods employed were of necessity indirect and the material gathered susceptible to differences of interpretation. Moreover, we fully recognize that the whole question of trial by jury is one that raises strong emotions and that views about the value of the jury are unlikely to be much affected one way or the other by the evidence of empirical research. Nevertheless, we think it better that such views be informed by the available evidence rather than allowed to pass in ignorance of it. The results of our inquiry may at first sight seem somewhat paradoxical in that they offer evidence both of basic weaknesses and of fundamental strengths in the system of trial by jury. Whilst it is important to bear in mind that our research is inevitably tentative in character, some of the results stand out so clearly that they cannot lightly be disregarded.

Much of the criticism of the trial system in England in recent years has been concerned with the sorts of defendant acquitted in the Crown Court and with the methods allegedly employed to secure an acquittal at all costs. As we have discussed in the previous chapter, some observers have alleged that the individual best able to secure an acquittal is the professional criminal, sometimes abetted by dishonest lawyers and that, even when such defendants are convicted, it may well be only because the jury is now empowered to bring in a majority verdict. Our analysis of the criminal histories of professional criminals for both Birmingham and London demonstrated how such a belief may have arisen. It appeared from our research that professional crooks did on occasion make apprehension extremely difficult; that they were sometimes successful in minimizing the seriousness of the charges brought; that they had, as against their non-professional counterparts, secured a disproportionate share of previous acquittals; and that they had managed, often with considerable success, to avoid for long periods the imposition of harsh penal sanctions. It is also of significance that, when any allegation of malpractice was levelled against lawyers, it was made (with only one exception) against a lawyer who was acting on behalf of a professional criminal. Although police concern appeared therefore to have some justification, closer investigation showed that concern to have been largely misplaced. The success of professional criminals was often more apparent than real. In the trials that we examined, professional criminals were not acquitted with any frequency and they were only rarely acquitted in questionable circumstances. On conviction, professional criminals as a whole received heavier sentences than other groups, probably because they had on average longer criminal records. The evidence suggests, therefore, that though the police undoubtedly face great difficulties in apprehending and charging many defendants within this group, this does not mean that the criminal justice system is at the mercy of the professional crook. There may well be some lawyers in London who are prepared to engage in dubious or dishonest practices on behalf of the well-heeled professional criminal, but there are always likely to be insuperable difficulties of proof in establishing whether or not this is the case. However that may be, we found little evidence to justify amending rules of evidence or procedure on the basis of the supposed ability of professional criminals to exploit the system: the great weight of the evidence is in fact to the contrary.

The evidence relating to jury composition was in certain respects less clear-cut. If Birmingham is representative of other Crown Court centres, the ideal of the jury being a cross-section of the community at large is only partially achieved. As we have seen in Chapter 6, the jury is broadly representative of the community in terms of age and social class, but unrepresentative in terms of sex and race. Although the sex imbalance is partly accounted for by informal summoning procedures, there is no good explanation for the extreme under-representation of non-British citizens. In one sense this imbalance may not matter overmuch, for there appeared to be (so far as we were able to test) no consistent relationships between the composition of the jury and its verdict. But there is another principle here that is also important: that justice must be seen to be done. In other words, the belief that there is, in the eyes of certain groups, a direct relationship between the composition of the jury and the quality of justice it will dispense is itself a strong argument for ensuring that the make-up of the jury offers no grounds for doubting its impartiality.[1] Where the jury panel is manifestly unrepresentative of the wider community, doubts can be quite reasonably raised. This difficulty might be overcome by alterations to present selection procedures. As long ago as 1913, the Mersey Committee recommended that jurors should be chosen according to some mechanical and uniform system.[2] Consideration to this question was later given by the Morris Committee (1965) who found considerable variation from place to place in the methods of selection used by summoning officers, and they concluded that the method chosen should in the last resort be left to the individual summoning officer. The Committee nevertheless took the view that the fairest basis would be selection at random and they recommended that summoning officers should be encouraged to make use of computers and other modern aids.[3] The sort of imbalances in jury composition that we have noted in Birmingham can only fuel (if they do not actually create) the lack of confidence felt amongst certain groups in the impartiality of justice.

Although there was no evidence from our study to suggest any relationship between the composition of the jury and the verdict returned, it is clear none the less that juries in both Birmingham and London were thought by respondents to have reached wrong or questionable conclusions on the evidence with a surprising frequency. Moreover, when we examined the

[1] As regards the views of racial minorities, see Dashwood (1972). He argues for improving the system of screening jurors and concludes that, at present, there 'is no way of reassuring those members of the coloured community whose real sense of insecurity, unfounded though it may be, has led to the demand for all-black juries'(p. 94).

[2] The Mersey Committee (1913) Cd. 6817, para. 251.

[3] Op. cit. paras. 195–8, 234–5. See also the discussion in Cornish (1968) at pp. 41–3, 255–6.

cases that respondents regarded as doubtful, it appeared to us that there was not, save with a few exceptions, any obvious explanation for the verdicts in question. In respect of a few acquittals, it might be said that the jury's verdict was primarily conditioned by its sympathy for the defendant or its antipathy towards the victim. Furthermore, some questionable convictions can possibly be explained on the basis of sympathy with the victim or prejudice against the defendant. But the performance of the jury did not always appear to accord with the principle underlying the trial system in England that it is better to acquit those who are probably guilty than to convict any who are possibly innocent. On the contrary, the jury appeared on occasion to be over-ready to acquit those who were probably guilty and insufficiently prepared to protect the possibly innocent. Both these tendencies may lead one to reflect upon some of the basic assumptions made about the fair and proper administration of criminal justice. They indicate also more immediate concerns, some of which cannot be easily remedied.

The most disturbing finding to emerge from our research is, in our view, that relating to questionable convictions. It is well known, of course, that, despite the high burden of proof upon the prosecution in criminal cases, the operation of the judicial system occasionally results in the conviction of innocent defendants. Nor should this necessarily cause general disquiet: as Williams (1975) put it: 'It is unpalatable to contemplate the conviction of a single innocent defendant. But some risk must be run, because you cannot have a system of criminal trial without running some risk of a miscarriage of justice.' (p. 194.) Having said this, it is hard to view with equanimity the degree of risk that the present system seems to involve for the possibly innocent. According to the measure we adopted in Chapter 5, at least 5 per cent of those convicted by jury were said to have been convicted in doubtful circumstances. Moreover, the offences in question were far from trivial, a majority of the defendants receiving immediate custodial sentences. It is no adequate answer to point to current appeals procedures, for only two applications for leave to appeal against conviction were entered in this group of cases in Birmingham and both were refused. That the Court of Appeal is reluctant, save on a point of law or where there has been an irregularity in the course of the trial, to interfere with a jury's verdict cannot be doubted. If the reason for the Court's reluctance is a general confidence in the precision of jury trial or a belief that jury waywardness operates only to the advantage of the defendant, then it is perhaps time to reassess this assumption. The low proportion of defendants making applications for leave to appeal cannot be explained simply in terms of the pessimistic outlook of defendants or of their legal advisers.[4] Amongst the cases of questionable conviction in Birmingham, the defendants and their lawyers (sometimes even with the open or tacit support of the prosecution and the judge) wished to enter an appeal but decided after careful consideration that this would not be worth while. The truth is that the infrequency of appeals in these cases reflects a realistic appraisal of an appeals procedure which inhibits, except on technical grounds, an effective review of the question of guilt. That the jury gives no reasons for its verdict might itself prevent any widening of the grounds for an appeal, but in our judgment, until these grounds are widened and until the Court of Appeal demonstrates a much greater willingness to review cases where the jury has come to a questionable determination on the evidence, the doubtful conviction of a disturbing proportion of those charged with serious offences will remain an unavoidable by-product of the jury system.

If the issues thrown up by questionable convictions give rise to some dismay, those relating to questionable acquittals might be thought to be less disturbing. It has always been a fundamental principle of the English trial system that, if there is to be any bias, it is better to err on the side of acquitting the guilty. Seen in this way, the wrongful acquittal of some defendants is a small price to pay for safeguarding the overwhelming majority. This view has also been bolstered by the belief that wrongful acquittals are only likely to be wrongful in the sense of being contrary to the letter of the law but generally justifiable on extra-legal grounds. As we have discussed in Chapter 4, the acquittals we have classified as questionable seemed to us only exceptionally justifiable on equitable grounds, and they involved serious as well as trivial offences. However these cases are viewed, we believe the evidence to be sufficiently strong to

[4] Cf. Bottoms and McClean (1976) at pp. 177–83.

shake the dogmatic and complacent attitudes that tend to characterize opinions about the jury system. Before we consider some other implications of our study, it is important to set the results in perspective.

Trial by jury is now only a small part of our criminal justice system. No more than about one in twenty of those eligible to be tried by jury are so tried. In fact, in 1976, 85 per cent of those whose cases could have been tried by jury in England and Wales were dealt with in the lower courts and a majority of the remainder pleaded guilty in the Crown Court.[5] Furthermore, we for our part remain firmly convinced that the number of serious miscarriages produced by jury trial is, in numerical terms at least, of slight significance compared to the number of injustices encountered in those cases in which defendants are induced to plead guilty following some form of plea bargaining or other form of negotiated plea settlement.[6] Indeed, our analysis of the results of jury trials in both Birmingham and London indicates that, in almost six cases out of seven, there was no serious complaint about the jury's verdict from most of the respondents we contacted. It is apparent, therefore, that the number of questionable outcomes we have described in this book represents no more than a tiny fraction of all cases that pass through the criminal courts. Nevertheless, since jury trial as a rule involves serious criminal offences and since trial by jury is usually held out as the ideal mode of trial, its performance must be judged according to high standards.

Looking at the findings of our research, it is clear that we have classified considerably more jury verdicts as questionable than any other researcher has done, yet we have found it exceptionally difficult to find any distinctive patterns in the results obtained. In most respects, the questionable cases appear to represent a rough cross-section of the sample as a whole. Taken together, the questionable outcomes do not appear to be more serious, or more trivial, than other cases in the sample; they do not by and large involve defendants who are much different from other defendants in the sample. We

[5] See Home Office, *Criminal Statistics for England and Wales, 1976* (Cmnd. 6909), Table 4.1.

[6] Our reasons for this belief are dealt with at length in Baldwin and McConville (1977a).

could find no real support for the many explanations that have been put forward over the years to explain jury waywardness. So we could not, for example, explain the questionable outcomes in terms of the social composition of the jury; we could see little evidence of jury equity or of juries disliking particular laws; it did not seem that professional criminals were often able to secure wrongful acquittals. In short, almost no over-all patterns were evident[7] and no common factor or factors appeared to explain the questionable outcomes we encountered. The absence of any clear pattern in the results has one very important implication: since the unexpected verdicts occurred, as far as we could tell, entirely at random, there is nothing in the findings that would help one *predict* either the sort of cases in which questionable verdicts are to be anticipated or the kind of juries most likely to deliver such verdicts. In other words, the findings do not suggest any immediate way in which the imprecision of the present system can be greatly improved.

It must always be remembered that empirical research on questions of this kind must be primarily concerned with the competence of the jury in arriving at a just outcome and that this is only one of the jury's functions. One must not lose sight of the fact that the jury does serve a political function, both in involving laymen in the administration of justice and in acting in certain circumstances as a real safeguard against oppressive behaviour.[8] So although serious criticism may be levelled against the jury on the grounds of arbitrariness, prejudice, and the like, one may nevertheless state with confidence that the very unpredictability of the institution is the surest evidence of its genuine independence. As we indicated in Chapter 1, research can only illuminate that part of the jury's function which is concerned with the accuracy of its decisions, and then only in narrow terms. It is difficult to see how research could usefully be conducted into its political functions, but these functions are no less important because of that.[9]

[7] We discussed in Chapter 5 the over-representation of black defendants amongst the group of cases classified as questionable convictions. Given the small number of cases involved, however, even this pattern must be regarded as tentative in nature.
[8] See on this particularly Blackstone (1830); Devlin (1956) at p. 164; Emmet (1974); and Dashwood (1974).
[9] See generally Abraham (1968) Chapter 3; Note, *Columbia Law Review* (1969); and Erlanger (1970).

Our concern has been, then, not with the political functions of the jury, but with the limited question of its competence. Much of the evidence presented is of a qualitative nature and it is a matter of individual judgment whether such evidence is sufficiently strong and clear-cut to support our general conclusion that trial by jury is an arbitrary and unpredictable business. The evidence that we have presented in this book has shaken our own confidence in the system of trial by jury, though it is not our view that the jury should therefore be abolished. Decisions about the continuance of jury trial, or about modifications to existing procedures, are in the end political decisions and the researcher is in no better position than anyone else to make recommendations about such questions. Suffice it to say that we for our part no longer regard the jury with the sort of reverence it is customarily accorded by members of the legal profession, though only a fool would attempt to minimize the importance of its political and constitutional independence. Nevertheless we would argue that it is time that the deliberations of the jury were examined by researchers. The provocative view of Devons (1965) that 'if the jury is to remain part of the English legal system, it is just as well that its proceedings should remain secret' may be unduly cynical, but there seems to us no good reason why the jury room should continue to be inviolate. There can be few fields of scientific inquiry in which research is so heavily circumscribed and few institutions which are to such a degree protected as is the jury. Such reverence is becoming increasingly difficult to defend. We believe that our own inquiry has raised a sufficient number of important questions about the precision of trial by jury to justify giving researchers access to the jury room, if only under specified conditions.[10] The onus to demonstrate why this should not be done would appear now to lie with those who argue for its continued immunity from research. We believe that the air of mystery which surrounds the deliberations of juries needs finally to be swept away. Indeed, the results of the present inquiry suggest that it is in the interests of justice itself that this be done. Sir Robert Mark (1973) rightly observed that the public confidence which juries undoubtedly enjoy is based on almost

---

[10] This would not by any means resolve all difficulties: see letter in *The Times*, 15 November 1973, from McCabe and Cornish.

no evidence. This confidence may be misplaced and it is appropriate to question the complacency and shallow thinking which too often pass for informed opinion in discussions of legal institutions. We see nothing necessarily sacrosanct in the present system, and one need look no further afield than Scotland to observe a jury system quite different from the Anglo-American species.[11] The same is true of the jury system in other countries which provide a wealth of variation in terms of jury size, composition, and operating rules.[12] There are hints that consideration is being given to the introduction of six-member juries in England, despite the controversy that such juries have so far provoked in the United States,[13] though any proposal to modify the right to jury trial is bound to meet stiff resistance from many quarters.[14] This is not the place to discuss the relative merits of alternative modes of trial: our interest has necessarily been to examine the jury on its own terms rather than in relation to other forms of tribunal.

How far research can, or should, contribute to discussion of such changes remains contentious. There are some, of course, who would dismiss the value of all the research so far undertaken, because of the serious limitations under which all researchers have been compelled to operate. It would be foolish to seek to minimize the importance of these limitations, though

[11] Scottish juries consist of fifteen members and they can deliver verdicts according to straightforward majorities: see Sheehan (1975) at pp. 158–72 and Bell (1975). The Thomson Committee (1975) recommended, however, that in Scotland the number of jurors should be reduced to twelve and that the verdict should continue to be according to a simple majority (para. 51.13). The Committee's view was based on the curious ground that 'it would be a convenience to members of the public in that it would substantially reduce the number of people required for jury service' (para. 51.09).

[12] Having discussed in this book the instances in which judges expressed dissatisfaction with verdicts of juries, it is important to note that in many Continental countries, the judge actually sits with the jury to consider the verdict. The French jury system is discussed in Sheehan (1975) at p. 84, and those of Denmark and Austria in Kalven and Zeisel (1966) at pp. 516–20. An interesting discussion of the place of jury trial in certain Commonwealth countries is given in Mawer (1961). Other systems are discussed in Knittel and Seiler (1972); Burns (1973); Robinson (1973); and Molin (1975).

[13] On the whole, such 'mini-juries' have been unfavourably received in the United States. See, for instance, Walbert (1971); Brady (1972); Ball (1972); Ashman and McConnell (1973); Rosenblatt and Rosenblatt (1973); Zeisel and Diamond (1974); Lempert (1975); Saks (1977); and Van Dyke (1977).

[14] The proposals of the James' Committee (1975) to restrict a defendant's right to opt for trial by jury in certain cases involving theft were very severely criticized, both inside and outside Parliament. In the result, the relevant sections of the Bill had to be removed.

we think it would be equally dangerous to dismiss all the available evidence on these grounds. The results that we have presented do not necessarily demonstrate that trial by jury produces an insupportable level of injustice: nor should they be taken to show the opposite. It may be the case that the system reaches a right and just determination as often as can reasonably be expected of any tribunal and that we must live with a proportion of failures. The results of empirical research do not in the end obviate the need for value judgments, but such evidence ought to compel the protagonists in the debate to define the issues with greater clarity and discrimination. In future debates, it seems to us that opponents of trial by jury will have to contend with the fact that the jury seems to enjoy the considerable confidence of the public; it appears to return verdicts that are generally deemed reasonable by judges, lawyers, and the police; and, so far as one can tell, it successfully maintains its political and constitutional independence. On the other hand, defenders of the jury must take account of the fact that the ideal of the jury as a representative cross-section of the community is only partially reflected in its actual composition; that its verdicts are with some frequency highly questionable in character; that its capriciousness is likely both to prejudice the innocent and to benefit the guilty; and that there is no obvious corrective for its unpredictability.

BIBLIOGRAPHY

H. J. ABRAHAM *The Judicial Process*, Oxford University Press (1968).

F. ADLER 'Socio-economic Factors Influencing Jury Verdicts' *New York University Review of Law and Social Change* vol. 3 (1973) pp. 1–10.

R. ARENS, D. D. GRANFIELD, and J. SUSMAN 'Jurors, Jury Charges and Insanity' *Catholic University of America Law Review* vol. 14 (1965) pp. 1–28.

A. ASHMAN and J. McCONNELL 'Trial by Jury: The New Irrelevant Right?' *South Western Law Journal* vol. 27 (1973) pp. 436–53.

Association of Chief Police Officers 'Trial by Jury' *New Law Journal* vol. 116 (1966) pp. 928–9.

J. BALDWIN 'The Social Composition of the Magistracy' *British Journal of Criminology* vol. 16 (1976) pp. 171–4.

J. BALDWIN and M. McCONVILLE 'The Acquittal Rate of Professional Criminals: A Critical Note' *Modern Law Review* vol. 37 (1974) pp. 439–43.

J. BALDWIN and M. McCONVILLE *Negotiated Justice* Martin Robertson (1977a).

J. BALDWIN and M. McCONVILLE 'Guilty Pleas and the Risk to the Innocent—What is the Public Interest?' *Justice of the Peace* vol. 141 (1977b) pp. 621–3.

J. BALDWIN and M. McCONVILLE 'Patterns of Involvement Amongst Lawyers in Contested Cases in the Crown Court' *New Law Journal* vol. 127 (1977c) pp. 1040–1.

J. BALDWIN and M. McCONVILLE 'The New Home Office Figures on Pleas and Acquittals—What sense do they make?' *Criminal Law Review* (1978a) pp. 196–201.

J. BALDWIN and M. McCONVILLE 'The Influence of the Sentencing Discount in Inducing Guilty Pleas' in J. BALDWIN and A. K. BOTTOMLEY (ed.) *Criminal Justice: Selected Readings* Martin Robertson (1978b) pp. 116–28.

J. BALDWIN and M. McCONVILLE 'The Legal Profession and the Politics of Research' in R. LUCKHAM (ed.) *Law and Social Enquiry: Case Histories of Research* International Centre for Law in Development (forthcoming 1978c).

J. BALDWIN and M. McCONVILLE 'The Exercise of the Right to Silence' (forthcoming 1979).

A. W. BALL 'Changes in the Criminal Jury' *Mississippi Law Journal* vol. 43 (1972) pp. 214–27.

Z. BANKOWSKI and G. MUNGHAM 'The Jury in the Legal System' in P. CARLEN (ed.) *The Sociology of Law* University of Keele Sociological Review Monograph (1976) pp. 202–25.

D. BARBER and G. GORDON *Members of the Jury* Wildwood House (1976).

H. S. BECKER 'Whose side are we on?' *Social Problems* vol. 14 (1967) pp. 239–47.

T. L. BECKER *Comparative Judicial Politics* Rand–McNally (1970).

T. L. BECKER, D. C. HILDUM, and K. BATEMAN 'The Influence of Jurors'

136 BIBLIOGRAPHY

Values on their Verdicts: A Courts and Politics Experiment' *Southwestern Social Science Quarterly* vol. 46 (1965) pp. 130–40.

E. N. BEISER 'Are Juries Representative?' *Judicature* vol. 57 (1973) pp. 194–9.

S. E. BELL 'Special Features of Criminal Trial by Jury in Scotland' in N. WALKER (ed.) *The British Jury System* Cambridge (1975) pp. 100–3.

G. BERMANT, M. McGUIRE, W. McKINLEY, and C. SALO 'The Logic of Simulation in Jury Research' *Criminal Justice and Behaviour* vol. 1 (1974) pp. 224–33.

W. BEVAN, R. S. ALBERT, P. R. LOISEAUX, P. N. MAYFIELD, and G. WRIGHT 'Jury Behaviour as a Function of the Prestige of the Foreman and the Nature of his Leadership' *Journal of Public Law* vol. 7 (1958) pp. 419–49.

SIR WILLIAM BLACKSTONE *Commentaries on the Laws of England* (4 vols.) 17th Edition (1830).

V. R. BOEHM 'Mr. Prejudice, Miss Sympathy, and the Authoritarian Personality: An Application of Psychological Measuring Techniques to the Problem of Jury Bias' *Wisconsin Law Review* vol. 3 (1968) pp. 734–47.

E. M. BORCHARD *Convicting the Innocent* Plenum Publishing Co. (1970).

R. BOSHIER and D. JOHNSON 'Does Conviction Affect Employment Opportunities?' *British Journal of Criminology* vol. 14 (1974) pp. 264–8.

A. E. BOTTOMS and J. D. McCLEAN *Defendants in the Criminal Process* Routledge and Kegan Paul (1976).

A. E. BOTTOMS and M. A. WALKER 'The American Jury: A Critique' *Journal of the American Statistical Association* vol. 67 (1972) pp. 773–9.

R. M. BRADY 'The Jury: Is it viable?' *Suffolk University Law Review* vol. 6 (1972) pp. 897–918.

G. BRAND, G. WRIGHT, and R. E. SIESWERDA 'The Jury Looks at Trial by Jury' *Journal of the American Judicature Society* vol. 31 (1947) pp. 105–8.

R. BRANDON and C. DAVIES *Wrongful Imprisonment: Mistaken Convictions and their Consequences* Allen and Unwin (1973).

D. W. BROEDER 'The Functions of the Jury: Facts or Fictions?' *University of Chicago Law Review* vol. 21 (1954) pp. 386–424.

D. W. BROEDER 'The Negro in Court' *Duke Law Journal* vol. 19 (1965a) pp. 19–31.

D. W. BROEDER 'Occupational Expertise and Bias as Affecting Juror Behaviour: A Preliminary Look' *New York University Law Review* vol. 40 (1965b) pp. 1079–1100.

D. W. BROEDER 'Previous Jury Trial Service Affecting Juror Behaviour' *Insurance Law Journal* (1965c) pp. 138–43.

D. W. BROEDER 'The Importance of the Scapegoat in Jury Trial Cases: Some Preliminary Reflections' *Duquesne Law Review* vol. 4 (1966) pp. 513–25.

W. N. BROOKS and A. N. DOOB 'Justice and the Jury' *Journal of Social Issues* vol. 33 (1975) pp. 171–82.

R. BUCKHOUT 'Jury without Peers: An Overview of Social Science Research on Juries in Criminal Trials' Centre for Responsive Psychology monograph (1973).

P. T. BURNS 'A Profile of the Jury System in New Zealand' *Western Australia Law Review* vol. 11 (1973) pp. 105–10.

K. CARLSON, A. HALPER, and D. WHITCOMB *One Day/One Trial Jury System* National Institute of Law Enforcement and Criminal Justice (1977).

W. J. CHAMBLISS (ed.) *Crime and the Legal Process* McGraw-Hill (1969).

W. J. CHAMBLISS and R. D. SEIDMAN *Law, Order, and Power* Addison–Wesley (1971).

E. CLARKE 'The Selection of Juries, Qualification for Service and the Right of Challenge' in N. WALKER (ed.) *The British Jury System* Cambridge (1975) pp. 46–9.

R. V. G. CLARKE 'Penal Policy-Making and Research in the Home Office' in N. WALKER (ed.) *Penal Policy-Making in England* Cambridge (1977) pp. 115–26.

Note, Columbia Law Review, 'Trial by Jury in Criminal Cases, *Columbia Law Review* vol. 69 (1969) pp. 420–71.

M. J. CONNELLY 'Jury Duty—the Juror's View' *Judicature* vol. 55 (1971) pp. 118–21.

H. H. A. COOPER 'Plea-Bargaining: A Comparative Analysis' *New York University Journal of International Law and Politics* vol. 5 (1972) pp. 427–48.

P. H. CORBOY 'From the Bar' in R. J. SIMON (ed.) *The Jury System in America* Sage Publications (1975) pp. 181–95.

W. R. CORNISH *The Jury* Allen Lane (1968).

W. R. CORNISH 'Qualifications for Jury Service' *Criminal Law Review* (1973) pp. 24–6.

D. R. CRESSEY *Criminal Organisation* Heinemann (1972).

Criminal Law Revision Committee *Evidence (General) 11th Report* (1972) Cmnd. 4991.

J. CROFT *Research in Criminal Justice* Home Office Research Study, No. 44 H.M.S.O. (1978).

R. CROSS 'The Behaviour of the Jury: A Comment' *Criminal Law Review* (1967) pp. 575–7.

S. DASH 'Cracks in the Foundation of Criminal Justice' *Illinois Law Review* vol. 46 (1951) pp. 385–406.

A. DASHWOOD 'Juries in a Multi-racial Society' *Criminal Law Review* (1972) pp. 85–94.

A. DASHWOOD 'The Jury and the Angry Brigade' *Western Australia Law Review* vol. 11 (1974) pp. 245–55.

LORD DEVLIN *Trial by Jury* Stevens (1956).

LORD DEVLIN *The Criminal Prosecution in England* Oxford University Press (1960).

Devlin Committee *Evidence of Identification in Criminal Cases* H.M.S.O. (1976).

E. DEVONS 'Serving as a Juryman in Britain' *Modern Law Review* vol. 28 (1965) pp. 561–70.

A. DICKEY 'The Jury and Trial by One's Peers' *Western Australia Law Review* vol. 11 (1974) pp. 205–29.

LORD DU PARCQ *Aspects of Law* Address to the Holdsworth Club, University of Birmingham (1948).

S. J. ELGROD and J. D. M. LEW 'Acquittals—A Statistical Exercise' *New Law Journal* (1973) pp. 1104–6.

R. P. Emmet 'The Need for a Scientific Study of the Jury's Deliberative Process' *The Alabama Lawyer* vol. 35 (1974) pp. 97–103.

H. S. Erlanger 'Jury Research in America: Its Past and Future' *Law and Society Review* vol. 4 (1970) pp. 345–70.

W. Forsyth *History of Trial By Jury* London (1852).

J. Frank *Law and the Modern Mind* Coward–McCann (1930).

J. Frank *The Courts on Trial* Princeton University Press (1949).

J. Frank and B. Frank *Not Guilty* Victor Gollancz (1957).

M. Fried, K. J. Kaplan, and K. W. Klein 'Jury Selection: An Analysis of Voir Dire' in R. J. Simon (ed.) *The Jury System in America* Sage Publications (1975) pp. 49–66.

C. A. Friloux 'Another View from the Bar' in R. J. Simon (ed.) *The Jury System in America* Sage Publications (1975) pp. 219–31.

A. Fry *Memoirs of Sir Edward Fry* Oxford (1921).

General Council of the Bar *Evidence in Criminal Cases: Memorandum on the 11th Report of the Criminal Law Revision Committee: Evidence (General)* (1973).

J. Goldman, K. A. Maitland, and P. L. Norton 'Psychological Aspects of Jury Performance' *Journal of Psychiatry and Law* vol. 3 (1975) pp. 367–80.

J. H. Goldthorpe and K. Hope *The Social Grading of Occupations* Oxford University Press (1974).

D. S. Greer 'Anything but the Truth? The Reliability of Testimony in Criminal Trials' *British Journal of Criminology* vol. 11 (1971) pp. 131–54.

E. Griew 'The Behaviour of the Jury—A Review of the American Evidence' *Criminal Law Review* (1967) pp. 555–86.

T. L. Grisham and S. F. Lawless 'Jurors Judge Justice: A Survey of Criminal Jurors' *New Mexico Law Review* vol. 3 (1973) pp. 352–63.

J. Hale 'Juries: The West Australian Experience' *Western Australia Law Review* vol. 11 (1973) pp. 99–104.

Lord Halsbury 'Trial by Jury' *Law Journal* vol. 38 (1903) p. 469.

W. H. Hammond and E. Chayen *Persistent Criminals* H.M.S.O. (1963).

R. Hartshorne 'Jury Verdicts: A Study of their Characteristics and Trends' *American Bar Association Journal* vol. 35 (1949) pp. 113–17.

B. T. Head 'Confessions of a Juror' *Federal Rules Decisions* vol. 44 (1969) pp. 330–8.

J. L. Heberling 'Conviction Without Trial' *Anglo-American Law Review* vol. 2 (1973) pp. 428–72.

C. Hendrick and D. R. Shaffer 'Murder: Effects of Number of Killers and Victim Mutilation on Simulated Jurors' Judgments' *Bulletin of the Psychonomic Society* vol. 6 (1975) pp. 313–16.

P. J. Hermann 'Occupations of Jurors as an Influence on their Verdict' *The Forum* vol. 5 (1970) pp. 150–5.

J. G. Hervey 'The Jurors Look at our Judges' *Oklahoma Bar Journal* (1947) pp. 1508–13.

H. M. Hoffman and J. Brodley 'Jurors on Trial' *Missouri Law Review* vol. 17 (1952) pp. 235–51.

Home Office Statistical Department 'Acquittal Rates at the Crown Court January–June 1974' in N. Walker (ed.) *The British Jury System* Cambridge (1975) pp. 50–2.

R. HOOD *Sentencing the Motoring Offender* Heinemann (1972).

SIR TRAVERS HUMPHREYS *Criminal Days* Hodder and Stoughton (1946).

R. M. HUNTER 'Law in the Jury Room' *Ohio State University Law Journal* vol. 2 (1935) pp. 1–19.

R. M. JACKSON 'Jury Trial Today' in J. W. C. TURNER (ed.) *The Modern Approach to Criminal Law* Macmillan (1945) pp. 92–109.

James' Committee, *The Distribution of Criminal Business between the Crown Court and the Magistrates' Court* Cmnd. 6323 (1975).

R. M. JAMES 'Jurors' Assessment of Criminal Responsibility' *Social Problems* vol. 7 (1959a) pp. 58–69.

R. M. JAMES 'Status and Competence of Jurors' *American Journal of Sociology* vol. 64 (1959b) pp. 563–70.

R. M. JAMES 'Jurors' Evaluation of Expert Psychiatric Testimony' *Ohio State Law Journal* vol. 21 (1960) pp. 75–95.

SIR IVOR JENNINGS *The Law and the Constitution* (5th Edition) University of London Press (1959).

C. W. JOINER 'From the Bench' in R. J. SIMON (ed.) *The Jury System in America* Sage Publications (1975) pp. 145–57.

Note, Journal of Criminal Law and Criminology 'The Exclusion of Young Adults from Juries: A Threat to Jury Impartiality' *Journal of Criminal Law and Criminology* vol. 66 (1975) pp. 150–64.

Justice Report *Home Office Reviews of Criminal Convictions* (1968).

M. R. KADISH and S. H. KADISH 'The Institutionalisation of Conflict: Jury Acquittals' *Journal of Social Issues* vol. 27 (1971) pp. 199–217.

H. KALVEN 'The Dignity of the Civil Jury' *Virginia Law Review* vol. 50 (1964) pp. 1055–72.

H. KALVEN and H. ZEISEL *The American Jury* Boston: Little Brown (1966).

H. KALVEN and H. ZEISEL 'A Rejoinder to Bottoms and Walker's Critique' *Journal of the American Statistical Association* vol. 67 (1972) p. 779.

I. R. KAUFMAN 'A Fair Jury—The Essence of Justice' *Judicature* vol. 51 (1967) pp. 88–92.

E. KENNEBECK 'From the Jury Box' in R. J. SIMON (ed.) *The Jury System in America* Sage Publications (1975) pp. 235–50.

E. KNITTEL and D. SEILER 'The Merits of Trial by Jury: Some Aspects of English Jury Trial and Continental Modes of Trial' *Cambridge Law Journal* (1972) pp. 316–25.

C. KRAMER 'The Psychology of a Jury Trial' *The Practical Lawyer* vol. 16 (1970) pp. 61–72.

D. LANDY and E. ARONSON 'The Influence of the Character of the Criminal and his Victim on the Decisions of Simulated Jurors' *Journal of Experimental Social Psychology* vol. 5 (1969) pp. 141–52.

R. O. LEMPERT 'Uncovering "Non-discernible" Differences: Empirical Research and the Jury-size Cases' *Michigan Law Review* vol. 73 (1975) pp. 643–708.

D. J. McBARNET 'Pre-trial Procedures and the Construction of Conviction' in P. CARLEN (ed.) *The Sociology of Law* University of Keele Sociological Review Monograph (1976) pp. 172–201.

S. McCabe and R. Purves *The Jury at Work* Oxford University Penal Research Unit: Blackwell (1972).

S. McCabe 'Jury Research in England and the United States' *British Journal of Criminology* vol. 14 (1974) pp. 276–9.

S. McCabe 'Discussions in the Jury Room: Are they like this?' in N. Walker (ed.) *The British Jury System* Cambridge (1975) pp. 22–8.

S. McCabe and R. Purves *The Shadow Jury at Work* Oxford University Penal Research Unit: Blackwell (1974).

F. H. McClintock and N. H. Avison *Crime in England and Wales* Heinemann (1968).

M. McIntosh *The Organisation of Crime* Macmillan, London (1975).

J. A. Mack *The Crime Industry* Saxon House (1975).

J. A. Mack 'Full-time Major Criminals and the Courts' *Modern Law Review* vol. 39 (1976) pp. 241–67.

Sir Robert Mark *The Disease of Crime: Punishment or Treatment* London: Royal Society of Medicine (1972).

Sir Robert Mark *Minority Verdict* The 1973 Dimbleby Lecture, B.B.C. Publications (1973).

J. P. Martin and D. Webster *The Social Consequences of Conviction* Heinemann (1971).

R. K. Mawer 'Juries and Assessors in Criminal Trials in Some Commonwealth Countries: A Preliminary Survey' *International and Comparative Law Quarterly* vol. 10 (1961) pp. 892–8.

Mersey Committee *Jury Law and Practice* Cd. 6817 (1913).

Metropolitan Police District 'Acquittals in Contested Cases at the Higher Courts' *Law Society's Gazette*, 28 February 1973.

R. J. Miller 'The Woman Juror' *Oregon Law Review* vol. 2 (1922) pp. 41–51.

E. S. Mills 'A Statistical Study of Occupations of Jurors in a United States District Court' *Maryland Law Review* vol. 22 (1962) pp. 205–14.

E. S. Mills 'A Statistical Profile of Jurors in a United States District Court' *Arizona State Law Journal* (1969) pp. 329–39.

H. E. Mitchell and D. Byrne 'Effects of Jurors' Attitudes and Authoritarianism on Judicial Decisions' *Journal of Personality and Social Psychology* vol. 25 (1973) pp. 123–9.

D. W. Moffat 'As Jurors see a Lawsuit' *Oregon Law Review* vol. 24 (1945) pp. 199–207.

R. Moley 'The Vanishing Jury' *Southern California Law Review* vol. 2 (1928) pp. 97–127.

L. Molin 'Some Information about the Role of Lay Assessors in Swedish Courts' in N. Walker (ed.) *The British Jury System* Cambridge (1975) pp. 80–96.

E. M. Morgan *Some Problems of Proof Under the Anglo-American System of Litigation* Columbia University Press (1956).

M. J. Moriarty 'The Policy-Making Process: how it is seen from the Home Office' in N. Walker (ed.) *Penal Policy-Making in England* Cambridge (1977) pp. 129–45.

Morris Committee *Jury Service* (1965) Cmnd. 2627.

P. Morris *Prisoners and Their Families* Allen and Unwin (1965).

J. MORTON 'Trial by Blacklist' *New Law Journal* (1977) p. 280.

H. MÜNSTERBERG *Psychology and Social Sanity* Doubleday Page (1914).

S. NAGEL and L. WEITZMAN 'Sex and the Unbiased Jury' *Judicature* vol. 56 (1972) pp. 108–11.

D. NAPLEY 'The Jury System' *New Law Journal* (1966) pp. 1620–1.

D. NAPLEY 'The British Jury System: Guilty or Not Guilty?' *Law Society's Gazette*, 27 August 1975.

National Council for Civil Liberties *The Rights of Suspects* N.C.C.L. (1973).

C. NEMETH and R. H. SOSIS 'A Simulated Jury Study: Characteristics of the Defendant and the Jurors' *Journal of Social Psychology* vol. 90 (1973) pp. 221–9.

D. W. NEUBAUER *Criminal Justice in Middle America* General Learning Press (1974).

C. L. NEWMAN 'Trial by Jury: An Outmoded Relic?' *Journal of Criminal Law, Criminology and Police Science* vol. 46 (1955) pp. 512–18.

D. J. NEWMAN 'Pleading Guilty for Considerations: A Study of Bargain Justice' *Journal of Criminal Law, Criminology, and Police Science* vol. 46 (1956) pp. 780–90.

D. J. NEWMAN *Conviction: the Determination of Guilt or Innocence Without Trial* Boston: Little, Brown (1966).

L. NIZER 'The Art of the Jury Trial' *Cornell Law Quarterly* vol. 32 (1946) pp. 59–72.

G. D. NOKES 'The English Jury and the Law of Evidence' *Tulane Law Review* vol. 31 (1956) pp. 153–72.

B. S. OPPENHEIMER 'Trial by Jury' *University of Cincinnati Law Review* vol. 11 (1937) pp. 141–7.

J. PAUL 'Jerome Frank's Views on Trial by Jury' *Missouri Law Review* vol. 22 (1957) pp. 28–37.

R. POUND 'Law in Books and Law in Action' *American Law Review* vol. 44 (1910) pp. 12–24.

I. REID *Social Class Differences in Britain* Open Books (1977).

Release Lawyers' Group *Guilty Until Proved Innocent* (1973).

J. RHINE 'The Jury: A Reflection of the Prejudices of the Community' *Hastings Law Journal* vol. 20 (1969) pp. 1417–45.

M. T. W. ROBINSON 'The Jury System in Ireland' *Western Australia Law Review* vol. 11 (1973) pp. 111–19.

W. S. ROBINSON 'Bias, Probability, and Trial by Jury' *American Sociological Review* vol. 15 (1950) pp. 73–8.

E. J. B. ROSE *et al. Colour and Citizenship* Oxford University Press (1969).

A. M. ROSENBLATT and J. C. ROSENBLATT 'Six-member Juries in Criminal Cases: Legal and Psychological Considerations' *St. John's Law Review* vol. 47 (1973) pp. 615–33.

M. J. SAKS 'Social Scientists Can't Rig Juries' *Psychology Today* vol. 9 (1976) pp. 48–57.

M. J. SAKS *Jury Verdicts* Lexington Books (1977).

LORD SALMON *Crime and Punishment* Address to the Holdsworth Club, University of Birmingham (1974).

A. SANDERS 'Does Professional Crime Pay?—A Critical Comment on Mack' *Modern Law Review* vol. 40 (1977) pp. 553–60.

J. SCHULMAN, P. SHAVER, R. COLMAN, B. EMRICH, and R. CHRISTIE 'Recipe for a Jury' *Psychology Today* vol. 6 (1973) pp. 37–44.

A. P. SEALY 'What can be Learned from the Analysis of Simulated Juries?' in N. WALKER (ed.) *The British Jury System* Cambridge (1975) pp. 12–21.

A. P. SEALY and W. B. CORNISH 'Jurors and their Verdicts' *Modern Law Review* vol. 36 (1973a) pp. 496–508.

A. P. SEALY and W. R. CORNISH 'Juries and the Rules of Evidence: L.S.E. Jury Project' *Criminal Law Review* (1973b) pp. 208–23.

A. V. SHEEHAN *Criminal Procedure in Scotland and France* H.M.S.O. (1975).

R. J. SIMON *The Jury and the Defence of Insanity* Boston: Little, Brown (1967).

R. J. SIMON 'Beyond a Reasonable Doubt: An Experimental Attempt at Quantification' *Journal of Applied Behavioural Science* vol. 6 (1970) pp. 203–9.

R. J. SIMON and L. MAHAN 'Quantifying Burdens of Proof: A View from the Bench, the Jury and the Classroom' *Law and Society Review* vol. 5 (1971) pp. 319–30.

R. J. SIMON and P. MARSHALL 'The Jury System' in S. S. NAGEL (ed.) *The Rights of the Accused* Sage Publications (1972) pp. 211–33.

R. A. SKOCHDOPOLE 'Interrogating the Jury' *Nebraska State Bar Association Proceedings* (1966) pp. 533–9.

E. C. SNYDER 'Sex Role Differential and Juror Decisions' *Sociology and Social Research* (1971) pp. 442–8.

Note, Stanford Law Review 'A Study of the California Penalty Jury in First Degree-Murder Cases' *Stanford Law Review* vol. 21 (1969) pp. 1302–1497.

C. STEPHAN 'Selective Characteristics of Jurors and Litigants: Their Influence on Juries' Verdicts' in R. J. SIMON (ed.) *The Jury System in America* Sage Publications (1975) pp. 97–121.

F. L. STRODTBECK, R. M. JAMES, and C. HAWKINS 'Social Status in Jury Deliberations' *American Sociological Review* vol. 22 (1957) pp. 713–19.

F. L. STRODTBECK and R. D. MANN 'Sex Role Differentiation in Jury Deliberations' *Sociometry* vol. 19 (1956) pp. 3–11.

J. B. THAYER *A Preliminary Treatise on Evidence* Boston: Little, Brown (1898).

Thomson Committee *Criminal Procedure in Scotland (Second Report)* Cmnd. 6218 (1975).

A. DE TOCQUEVILLE *Democracy in America* Vintage Books (1960 edition).

J. H. VANDERZELL 'The Jury as a Community Cross-section' *Western Political Quarterly* vol. 19 (1966) pp. 136–49.

J. M. VAN DYKE 'The Jury as a Political Institution' *Catholic Lawyer* vol. 16 (1970) pp. 224–41.

J. M. VAN DYKE *Jury Selection Procedures: Our Uncertain Commitment to Representative Panels* Ballinger Publishing Co. (1977).

D. F. WALBERT 'The Effect of Jury Size on the Probability of Conviction: An Evaluation of *Williams* v *Florida*' *Case Western Law Review* vol. 22 (1971) pp. 529–54.

M. H. WALSH 'The American Jury: A Re-assessment' *Yale Law Journal* vol. 79 (1969) pp. 142–58.

W. B. WANAMAKER 'Trial by Jury' *University of Cincinnati Law Review* vol. 11 (1937) pp. 191–200.

H. P. WELD and E. R. DANZIG 'A Study of the Way in which a Verdict is Reached by a Jury' *American Journal of Psychology* vol. 53 (1940) pp. 518–36.

D. J. WEST *The Habitual Prisoner* Macmillan (1963).

P. A. WHITMAN 'Judicial Plea Bargaining' *Stanford Law Review* vol. 19 (1967) pp. 1082–92.

J. WIGMORE 'A Programme for the Trial of Jury Trial' *Journal of the American Judicature Society* vol. 12 (1929) pp. 166–71.

P. WILES 'Introduction: The New Criminologies' in P. WILES (ed.) *The Sociology of Crime and Delinquency in Britain: Vol. 2* Martin Robertson (1976) pp. 1–35.

G. WILLIAMS *The Proof of Guilt* Stevens (1963).

G. WILLIAMS 'The Work of Criminal Law Reform' *Journal of the Society of Public Teachers of Law* vol. 13 (1975) pp. 183–98.

M. E. WOLFGANG and T. SELLIN *The Measurement of Delinquency* Wiley (1964).

Note, Yale Law Journal 'The Case for Black Juries' *Yale Law Journal* vol. 79 (1970) pp. 531–50.

Note, Yale Law Journal 'Toward Principles of Jury Equity' *Yale Law Journal* vol. 83 (1974) pp. 1023–54.

M. ZANDER 'Legal Advice and Criminal Appeals: A Survey of Prisoners, Prisons, and Lawyers' *Criminal Law Review* (1972) pp. 132–73.

M. ZANDER 'Are Too Many Professional Criminals Avoiding Conviction?—A Study of Britain's Two Busiest Courts' *Modern Law Review* vol. 37 (1974a) pp. 28–61.

M. ZANDER 'The Acquittal Rate of Professional Criminals: A Reply' *Modern Law Review* vol. 37 (1974b) pp. 444–9.

M. ZANDER 'Acquittal Rates and Not Guilty Pleas: What do the Statistics Mean?' *Criminal Law Review* (1974c) pp. 401–8.

M. ZANDER 'Legal Advice and Criminal Appeals: The New Machinery' *Criminal Law Review* (1975) pp. 364–9.

M. ZANDER 'The Legal Profession and Academic Researchers—a Plea for a Better Relationship' *Law Society's Gazette*, 21 December 1977.

H. ZEISEL 'The Jury and the Court Delay' *Annals of the American Academy of Political and Social Science* vol. 320 (1960) pp. 46–52.

H. ZEISEL and S. S. DIAMOND '"Convincing Empirical Evidence" on the Six Member Jury' *University of Chicago Law Review* vol. 41 (1974) pp. 281–95.

H. ZEISEL, H. KALVEN, and B. BUCHHOLZ *Delay in the Court* Boston: Little, Brown (1959).

SUBJECT INDEX

AUTHOR INDEX